ACING CA

YOUR GUIDE TO NAVIGATING THE CA JOURNEY

KUSHAL LODHA

wyzr

Acing CA

Published by Wyzr Content Pvt. Ltd. 3053, Sobha Palladian, Yemalur Jn., Bengaluru - 560037

Author's note: Any references to historical events, real people, companies, brands, or real places are used for the purpose of education with no intent to malign or defame any such person, place, community, entity, group, or persons involved with any such event.

ISBN: 978-81-958168-8-0 (Paperback)
ISBN: 978-81-958168-9-7 (Ebook)

Editors: Yashraj Sharma, Prishita Tahilramani
Typeset in Adobe InDesign by Kajal Ahuja
Cover by Syed Rizvi

Printed and bound by Gopsons Papers Pvt. Ltd., Noida
First printing edition 2023

"Acquiring the most coveted CA qualification is a dream, a lot of hard work goes behind getting the results. This book exactly talks about that hard work and how you can stay ahead of the curve as well seize the opportunities that will shape your future."

Suresh Prabhu

Former Railway Minister | CA

"Kushal has successfully cleared his CA Exams with All India Ranks across all levels. This book talks about the study strategies that one should follow, and how to manage academics with articleship. It breaks several myths about the CA Course and will be a great value add to all the aspiring CAs of our nation."

TN Manoharan

Padma Shree | Chairman, IDBI Bank | Author - The Tech Phoenix | CA

"One of the many gems you will find in this book is: 'Don't let success go to your head. Let it go to your heart and then enjoy it like a child enjoys ice cream.' Kushal brings this childlike simplicity and frankness, not only to his writing but to everything he does. The book is his personal story, but it is told in such lucidity and unassuming way, it will charm you. It will become your story too. Most readers will finish it in one sitting. This book is a must-read for every aspirant to the career of a Chartered Accountant, and also for all others embarking on a career journey. The CA's profession is that of a conscience keeper. A CA is not supposed to be a bloodhound, but rather a gentle watchdog. Kushal's book brings out such and many other attributes of what it takes to succeed in this profession. He speaks from experience, not just bookish knowledge. At a young age, he has tasted the pinnacle of success, but he remains firmly grounded, and is eager to share his joy of learning with others."

Dr. Ajit Ranade

Former Chief Economist, Aditya Birla Group

"This book talks about the various opportunities for CAs in and outside India. This is a must-read for all the CA students and professionals wanting to know how they can leverage the degree of CA in their career ahead. Moreover, this book will act as a guiding light for all the students to prepare for their CA journey ahead."

Ashwin Damera

Founder, Eruditus | CA

"Kushal has put together a resource like none other on acing the CA exams. He has answered questions that every CA aspirant has, not just before signing up for the course, but at each stage... CPT, IPCC, Articleship, Final, and beyond. There could've been no one better than him in putting this together, and my heart warms to see how he has given his secrets away for everyone to learn from and emulate."

Sarthak Ahuja

CA, CS, CMA, BFIA, MBA (ISB gold medallist) | Author - Daily Coffee & Startup Fundraising

For Mom and Dad.
I'd be nothing without your
support and sacrifices.

CONTENTS

Foreword

Kushal Lodha's 'Acing CA' acts as a guiding light for aspiring Chartered Accountants and those who are in different stages of their CA exams. Kushal is deeply aware that the accountancy profession has undergone a transformational change over the last two to three decades. The stereotyped image of an introverted book-keeper has been replaced by that of well-rounded professionals who are expected to have a deep understanding of a company and provide operational insights and support.

Kushal informs his readers that clearing the CA exams is a formidable task with a qualifying rate of only 2-3%. However, he assuages that it is an achievable goal by incorporating the right strategies. Kushal deftly takes the reader on his journey and elucidates how he successfully became a CA and the reasons behind his unbridled motivation. What makes this book unique is that he is a young man who understands the challenges of the current generation and aptly advises prospective CAs on the sacrifices they need to make. From his personal experience he provides preparation techniques, and the art of prioritising time.

Importantly, he advises how to practically use the theoretical knowledge gained in this process. Kushal is honest and writes about how he was rejected from the various job interviews he gave when he was starting out. Despite initial apprehensions and self-doubt, Kushal persevered and finally got an offer from the respected Aditya Birla Group. Having gone through his internship and corporate job from a demanding work environment, he quickly learnt to adapt and operate in the real world. I am sure that his commitment to pursue his dreams will be highly inspirational for all the readers.

His trial by fire insights will be immensely beneficial to the reader. I personally believe that this is critical as the competition for obtaining jobs is immense as CAs are competing with MBAs and other professional degree holders who are now well versed in finance and the economy. To be successful, CAs need to develop requisite all-round skills in various other areas, besides accounting. CAs need to learn to raise their standards by being more flexible, lateral, and creative thinkers.

Kushal points out that many CAs after clearing their exams are under the wrong impression that they have reached the pinnacle of their achievement. However, Kushal rightly makes it clear that becoming a CA is just the beginning of the long road ahead. In my opinion, a CA needs to make a commitment to lifelong learning. A CA needs to continually stay abreast with regulatory changes and have analytical abilities to foresee the potential impact of such changes.

On a closing note, I wanted to convey that the essence of a CA is about strong integrity, ethics and accountability. Accountants have to be synonymous with fair and equitable governance. CAs must keep a vigilant eye and a transparent cover on the books of accounts of clients. The numerical, quantifiable criteria of financial reporting now needs to be substituted by qualitative output and performance indicators.

I want to congratulate Kushal for writing this pertinent and timely book. I wish him and 'Acing CA' my very best.

Deepak Parekh
Chairman, HDFC

Mumbai
February, 2023

1. A Little Backstory

My story began with someone's failure. A young boy, long back, would sit under the lamplight, sometimes with a 102-degree fever and a wet cloth tied around his head, studying for the approaching CA exams. Despite his dedication, he failed at them because luck wasn't on his side.

That boy was my father. The broken pieces of my father's dream to become a CA became the foundation stone for mine. After all, every parent in the world wants their child to go beyond what they have achieved in their lives. So I thought if I become a CA, I'd fulfill my father's unrealized dream.

My dad moved from Mumbai to Nashik in 1998 and

rented a small 1 BHK to figure out what he wanted to do next. I watched him build an entire real estate business from the ground up. Through his journey, I learned that skill is more important than a degree. His journey also taught me an important life lesson: to succeed at anything, you need the right mindset. I observed the hard work he put into his business, his never-give-up attitude after facing setbacks, and his courage and resilience to always come back stronger. Thanks to his mindset and hard work, things started to improve. We moved into a 3BHK that he bought and our lives improved significantly.

When I was in Grade 4, my parents had to make a decision about switching me to one of the best schools in Nashik. My sister, who was in Grade 8 at the time, also wanted to switch, but the fees were too high for both of us to attend it. She, being the more mature one, sacrificed for my sake. I didn't understand its significance then, but I now recognize how much of an impact it has had on my life. I'll never be able to thank her enough for that, and for all the other ways she has helped me reach my goals - including dropping me off for my after-school tuitions and cooking my favourite meals when our parents were away.

Today, she has her start-up where she sells customized footwear and handbags. I can't be more proud of her!

I wasn't a born topper. On the contrary, I was a notorious kid with a short temper and average academic capabilities. I hated failure right from my childhood even in little things. For instance, if I lost a game of carrom with my sister, I would jump on the carrom board and break it so that no one could play it subsequently. And I was foolishly, almost laughably short-tempered. Once, I had forgotten to turn off the fan in the kitchen and my dad turned it off without my knowledge. He probably forgot about it and casually asked me to turn it off. I went from my room to the kitchen to see that the fan was off already. I was infuriated. I thought I was being made fun of! In my fit of rage, I broke a beautiful flower vase that we had recently purchased. However, today, I'm a lot calmer and rarely get angry. All the steam was blown off in childhood.

~

My new school followed the IGCSE curriculum, which enabled me to explore a variety of extracurricular activities, such as debates and MUNs. I loved being involved in these activities a lot more than academics. Despite not being particularly good at them, I still participated and tried. I remember my first MUN, where I was so intimidated that I couldn't speak at all. However, I was determined not to give up, inspired by my dad's never-give-up attitude. The mirrors in the washroom bore witness to a fourteen-year-old boy nervously rehearsing his speech while pacing back and forth.

Although my parents were pleased that I was exploring different things with an intense determination, they were also concerned about the imbalance between academics and extracurricular activities.

School wasn't really a bed of roses. In 8th grade in 2011, I dreaded going to school because of the constant bullying I suffered from the rowdy kids in my class. I was extremely skinny with a *champu* hairdo and that made me an easy target for body shaming. I was also called a teacher's pet and accused of taking favours from them. Those bullies made my life miserable for that year.

Being the Co-curricular Activities (CCA) captain in Grade 8th, one of my responsibilities was to conduct the morning assembly prayers. I still remember that several seniors would always laugh when I conducted the assembly in front of 800 students. I used to literally shiver while holding the mic. My class teacher one day noticed my distress and offered me some words of wisdom. She introduced me to what I call as the lotus analogy.

A beautiful lotus, which is a center of attraction for everyone, grows in dirty water and amongst the mud. She asked me to be like the lotus, to focus on my development and ignore the mud around me. Why? Because I am the author of my own life. Throughout life, I will encounter people who try to pull me down. If I let them affect me, then I am giving away the authorship of my story. Was I ready to become a side character in my own life? No. So, I embedded this analogy in my mind. I started focusing more on myself and ignoring the bullies. I trained my ear for selective hearing, taking in only what benefits me and ignored the mud around. This analogy helped me develop a thick skin and it has been useful in various instances throughout my life.

~

My academic performance had suffered during this difficult period, and I had strayed further away from the expectations of my parents. As I was about to enter high school, my dad decided it was time to have a chat. He sat me down and conveyed clearly: he was happy with my progress in extracurricular activities, but he was concerned about my academics. At first, I didn't understand, and I was angry. Then, he explained that he didn't want me to excel in only academics and leave extracurricular activities, nor did he want me to excel in only extracurriculars and leave academics. Doing anything in excess and ignoring something else important are both bad. To lead a meaningful life, I needed to have balance. Just like how people sometimes lose their health in the pursuit of money, focusing entirely on extracurricular activities and not giving my academics the attention it needs is wrong. I understood what he said.

The lotus analogy, combined with my dad's pep talk, changed my perspective as I entered high school. I didn't abandon my extracurricular activities; I still played sports and took part in debates, but I also made time for my academics, studying for six hours a day. This approach led to progress in both my extracurriculars and academics. From a 9/10th rank in middle school, I stood 2nd in the 10th boards. I was also the captain of my school's under-14 cricket team. I was delighted with my progress, so I continued with the same approach. This approach also led to me becoming the national topper in Additional Mathematics and Accounting at A levels in my 12th board. It was during high school that I truly developed holistically.

What made me even happier was that the bullies who used to trouble me and call me names were the first to congratulate me. I didn't let them dictate my life and I rose above the mud to become the lotus. I made my dad proud by achieving the balance he taught me.

Remember one thing: You will meet thousands of people in your life going ahead, all different. Some will trouble you, some will motivate you, some will demean you, and some will uplift you! Choose the ones that will always be your anchor no matter how well you do in your life.

Ignore the naysayers! Just focus on the positive layers!

As I finished 10th, it was only natural to wonder, *what do I do next?*

2. Seeds of CA

What should I do next? Which stream should I choose? What do I want to do in college and in life? I experienced the same existential crisis that every student goes through after completing 10th grade. These questions lingered in my home. At first, I was uncertain. Although I had been exposed to the idea of becoming a Chartered Accountant (CA) since I was a child, I hadn't given it too much thought. It wasn't until I was about to finish 12th that I realized the potential of becoming a CA and decided to nurture the seeds that had been sown long back. But how did I come to this realization? There were several instances and signs that all culminated in this decision.

I have always been passionate about numbers. Both due to my family's Marwari heritage, but more because of the influence of my father's entrepreneurial journey. He would often explain his business to me in simple terms, so I could better understand it. As I grew older, we would have conversations about business and how the market works. I have seen his successes and failures and learned from both. Growing up in a family of entrepreneurs, I was exposed to the language of numbers from a young age. As I grew older, the business conversations became more insightful and interesting, and he would sometimes quiz me about business decisions based on some numbers that he'd throw at me. This further honed my love for numbers. I saw them not as random problems to solve in exams, but as real puzzles that actually made an impact on businesses.

I explored other fields like dancing, singing, drawing, karate, and chess too, but mom's attempts to get me to like them failed. They failed to excite me and challenge me and I quit them. I didn't want to waste my energy on something that I never liked. But the things I liked, I would do with utmost sincerity. One such thing was the abacus classes. I enjoyed them because, again, I loved playing with numbers. I found it a fascinating challenge to solve 10 questions about adding two-digit numbers in one minute. As I progressed through the levels of the abacus, the difficulty increased and my interest grew. Eventually, I was able to complete all the levels of the abacus.

Once I realized I loved mathematics, I had to decide which field to pursue. Maths is linked to both Commerce and Science, so I had to choose between PCM and Commerce. If I had been in CBSE or ICSE, this would have been a difficult decision. But luckily, IGCSE's liberal curriculum allowed me to study both Commerce and Science alongside Maths in my 11th and 12th. I was studying Physics, Maths, Accounting, Economics, and English. Soon, I realized that quantum physics and the laws of gravity were beyond me, so I dropped Physics in 12th. I was enjoying myself in the world of debit, credit, and accounting sheets and could see a future for myself in it. I didn't know what I wanted to do in life, but I knew I wanted to do something related to Maths and Finance.

Having narrowed it down to Mathematics and Finance, CA seemed like the best option available. Moreover, with my lack of clarity about what I wanted to become, doing CA would keep a lot of doors open while I figured out my true calling in parallel. I embraced the saying - "CA makes you the jack of all and a master of one" - and decided to put my eggs in this big basket.

Apart from all the objective reasoning, I still feel a big

reason to take up this course was the latent desire to fulfill my father's dream of becoming a CA. He could not do it but I wanted him to realize that dream through me. By fulfilling his dream, I was fulfilling mine.

Apart from my academic interests and my desire to fulfill dad's dream, the last contributing factor to the CA decision was the frugal financial habits I had inculcated since childhood. Once I started receiving my pocket money, I made my expense diary which I would update every day before going to sleep. In that diary, I noted down my daily expenses and how much I saved every month (if I saved any). Growing up, I still do that. The only difference is that the diary is replaced with an Excel sheet. I've shared a glimpse of it on the next page.

Finally, I needed to have the conviction to pursue an academically heavy degree like CA. It requires at least 5 gruesome years of your life with a low probability of passing all three levels to earn the degree. The selection rate for CA ranges from 3% to 20%. The passing rate is low even in the best of times. Only a few thousand qualify from the lakhs of candidates who try. So why did I set myself up for something whose probability of failure is so high?

The reasons were primarily two: low cost and high returns.

Sr. No.	Date	Particulars	Mode	Amount (Rs.)
244	20-11-2022	Dinner with Raju Vinayak	Cash	1,230
245	21-11-2022	Uber to Marico	Cash	267
246	21-11-2022	Uber to LP	Cash	250
247	21-11-2022	Ritik Videographer	GPay	5,000
248	21-11-2022	Podcast Mic	GPay	21,000
249	21-11-2022	Gas	Cash	1,350
250	21-11-2022	Flight ticket of Jaipur	GPay	11,923
251	22-11-2022	Uber to Taj Lands End	Cash	300
252	22-11-2022	Cab to LP	Cash	330
253	22-11-2022	Paid to CAI for Jinisha	GPay	4,898
254	22-11-2022	Twitter Management	GPay	4,000
255	22-11-2022	Coffee	Cash	50
256	23-11-2022	Coffee and Fries	Cash	180
257	26-11-2022	Coffee	Cash	50
258	26-11-2022	Facewash and Peanut Butter	Cash	425
259	26-11-2022	Dry Fruits	PayTM	1,223
260	26-11-2022	Coffee with Viren	Cash	100
261	28-11-2022	Cab to airport	Cash	260
262	28-11-2022	Cab to CarDekho	Cash	300
263	28-11-2022	Ice Cream	Cash	200
264	28-11-2022	Cab to airport	Cash	110
265	28-11-2022	Cab to LP	Cash	660
266	29-11-2022	Lamination of TN Manoharan Poen	Cash	30
267	29-11-2022	Cab to Taj	Cash	290
268	29-11-2022	Cab to LP	Cash	240
269	29-11-2022	Spotify Management	GPay	1,000
270	30-11-2022	Nimish Salary	GPay	10,000
271	30-11-2022	Sahil Salary	GPay	12,000
272	02-12-2022	Rent	GPay	41,600
273	02-12-2022	Pen	Cash	150
274	02-12-2022	Laundry	Cash	480
275	02-12-2022	Dinner with Subbu	GPay	1,200
276	04-12-2022	Pramod Salary	Cash	2,400
277	04-12-2022	Coffee with Samyak Kothari	Cash	150

My expenses as maintained on Excel

The cost of CA education is much lower than other courses, which meant my tangible investment would be less. Of course, the intangible investment in terms of time invested, hard work, consistency, and sacrifices would be very high, but it wasn't something I shied away from.

The total cost for doing the CA Course can be broken

down into following parts:

1. CA Foundation Registration – Rs. 9,000
2. CA Foundation classes – Rs. 25,000-50,000
3. CA Intermediate Registration – Rs. 18,000
4. CA Intermediate Classes – Rs. 80,000-1,00,000
5. ITT and OC – Rs. 15,000
6. GMCS and ITT – Rs. 28,000
7. CA Final Registration – Rs. 22,000
8. CA Final Classes – Rs. 1,00,000

Therefore, the total cost will approximately be Rs. 3,42,000 or max Rs. 3,50,000 on the higher end of the spectrum. You can recover this entire cost in less than a year in a job if you clear your examinations.

Moreover, Chartered Accountancy is one of the rare fields where the unemployment rate is zero and options are limitless. You could opt for a conventional career path like working in an MNC, or choose to build your own practice, or even become a teacher. The financial stability offered by the CA degree was worth the uncertainty for five years.

With a clear upside, CA seemed like a risk worth taking. It was a challenge and I always love a good challenge. My conviction was strong, and I knew I'd find a way to succeed.

My advice for folks stuck at this phase: Do what you feel is right for you! What is right for you may not be right for someone else. It's pointless to take a decision by comparing yourself to someone else. Everyone is dealing with different situations in life.

Listen to your heart and implement it through your mind.

3. Who Is CA Really For?

W*ho should pursue CA? Am I suited to the CA curriculum?* These are two questions I'm asked frequently. But before I address them, let me first remind you of the challenges so you can take an informed decision before taking the plunge.

Firstly, the CA program requires five years of commitment. You must be patient and consistent throughout this rather long duration and be willing to learn constantly. On top of it, the qualification rate for CA is notoriously low, and despite the efforts, there's no guarantee of a degree, unlike many other courses. Successfully cracking CA is a full-time pursuit and not a side hustle. If you're unwilling to be patient and hardworking for 5 years, you must seriously reconsider your options.

Having said that, it's also not as hard as it's sometimes made out to be. If you have the right systems and routines in place, your chances of qualification become extremely good irrespective of how naturally sharp you are.

Also, what makes CA worth the risk is its high return on investment. It's one of those rare professions where not a single person stays unemployed. Since it's hard and selective, it's a degree that gives you immense credibility and opens doors more easily. I experience it firsthand when I reach out to industry stalwarts who are Chartered Accountants, which have included the likes of Mr. Suresh Prabhu (Former Railway Minister), Dr. Niranjan Hiranandani (Chairman, Hiranandani Group), Mr. Nirmal Jain (Chairman, IIFL), and many more.

If you ask, what has CA given me? I'd hardly stop.

- My first paycheck, a stipend of ₹3,000 per month at just the age of 18 when I started my articleship!
- My first dream job in the Aditya Birla Group!
- An opportunity to start my content creation journey on YouTube!
- Interacting and learning directly from senior CA stalwarts like Dr. Niranjan Hiranandani, Mr. Nirmal Jain, Mr. Suresh Prabhu, Padma Shri TN Manoharan, and many more!

- Most importantly, tears of joy to my parents when my result was announced!

There is so much to thank CA for.

~

CA is surely a risk worth taking. But who should take this risk? The most important pre-requisite for pursuing CA is an interest in any area of finance - accounting, taxation, investment banking, auditing, vouching and verification, etc. If you're fascinated by any of these fields, you and the CA curriculum are a match made in heaven.

Students belong to one of these two types: ones who are clear about their future plans, and ones who are uncertain but have a general idea of what they want to pursue. If you're the former and envision yourself walking into MNCs like JP Morgan, Morgan Stanley, and Goldman Sachs in a crisp suit, briefcase in one hand and Starbucks coffee in the other as an investment banker or a private equity expert, then a CA degree can get you closer to your dream. All of these companies have certain programs which recruit CAs.

In general, CAs are high in demand for many finance-oriented MNC jobs like equity research, fund management, investment banking, private equity investing, venture capital, due diligence, valuations, portfolio management, and several other roles. Many top companies prefer CAs over other graduates for such roles because of their breadth and depth of knowledge across the spectrum of finance - equity markets, taxation, accounting, legal implications, etc. An MBA in Finance may help one understand some facets of these jobs, but CA equips one holistically, especially for hardcore finance roles.

If you're someone who's uncertain about where you want to be, then I'd repeat the main pre-requisite for pursuing CA: interest in at least some area of finance. Without it, there's no point even thinking about taking on such a course.

If you pass this criterion, then options for finance lovers also include certifications such as CFA and FRM which are relatively easier, yet I would keep CA above these. Why? As I mentioned earlier, the CA curriculum makes you the jack of all and master of one, which means you would have many more options open after the degree. Other courses are like specializations in a particular field. E.g., CFA will allow you to have a career as an investment banker or research analyst. Doing a course in Taxation will allow you to become a tax consultant. But a CA can do everything. So if you are confused, the CA degree offers you the most flexibility and maximum opportunities. It allows you the necessary bandwidth to figure out your life and career, and switch fields if necessary. So if you did your articleship as a tax consultant and realized you don't enjoy it, you can still explore other options after finishing the degree. Hence, if you love the world of finance but are unsure about the field, CA gives you the best foundation and the highest credibility.

~

But it doesn't end here. Let's move to the second burning question among aspirants: *Am I suited to the CA curriculum?*

There's a widespread misconception that only students with high academic scores in 11th and 12th can crack CA. However, I've seen a lot of 'good students' with over 90% in 12th fail in CA exams. On the other hand, I've also seen 'average students' who scored in 60s in 12th secure ranks in CA in their first attempts. In fact, a close friend of mine scored just about 70% in his boards but cleared CA on the very first attempt.

People forget that the school syllabus and the CA curriculum are vastly different and necessitate different approaches to success. Being a great student in school doesn't guarantee a CA degree, nor does being average in school set you up for failure.

There are several reasons for it. Passing CA, unlike school exams, can't be done with just a few weeks of effort. Many smart people who are accustomed to short sprints of success in school struggle in CA. Secondly, students also mature during the 5 years of CA. Many who were casual and insincere in school change for the good and perform exceptionally well. Anyone with a strong growth mindset is much likelier to succeed than someone with a fixed mindset who rests on their past laurels. My friend succeeded because he understood well the challenges posed by the CA curriculum and worked accordingly. He grew more patient and dedicated.

With this misconception cleared, let's get back to the question: who exactly is suited to the CA curriculum? Answer: *Intelligent people*.

Give your arched eyebrows a break and hear me out. I am not contradicting myself. When I say 'intelligent' I don't define it in terms of IQ. Benjamin Graham, in his book *The Intelligent Investor*, called intelligence a trait more of character than of the brain. It is a lot more about patience, discipline, and eagerness to learn. Ask yourself: who are you as a person? Are you patient and disciplined enough to follow a strict routine for 5 years? Are you willing to sacrifice some of the fun your peers pursuing other degrees would have? Are you willing to put in a little more effort for the sake of a better life and career ahead? If you are not right now, are you willing to learn and acquire these traits as you move forward?

The next critical trait is *consistency*. The vast CA syllabus necessitates long study hours - consistently and daily for 5 years. Pulling all-nighters just weeks before the exam without being diligent in the months before would guarantee failure. If you can stay patient, disciplined and consistent with your efforts for 5 years, I can assure you of not just success as a CA aspirant, but also in your career thereafter.

~

But how does one stay consistent? This is a question I've often been asked. The biggest enemy of consistency, I think, is social media and OTT platforms. Distraction kills consistency, and the sources of distraction today are Instagram, Facebook, Twitter, Netflix, YouTube, and the like. If you decide to take the CA plunge, you need to have your priorities set. Literally. Let me elaborate.

The key to being consistent is smart *time prioritization*. Number the tasks to complete in a day in order of their priority and go to them one by one. As a CA student, you'll have multiple subjects to grasp, an articleship to manage, some extra-curricular activities possibly, and other personal commitments from time to time. Time prioritization will allow you to multitask effectively. Remember, it's not about doing multiple tasks at once, but doing multiple tasks one by one in the right order of priority. I have always sworn by this mantra.

In this prioritization order, you should constantly have some time dedicated to distractions like Netflix and Instagram. Needless to say, it should be the least, even zero if possible. You cannot afford to spend hours daily on social media and mindlessly scroll through Instagram. Be cognizant of what distracts you and limit it to the least if you can't eliminate them. When I was in your shoes, I had shut myself off from all social media.

Even though I'm a creator myself today, I'd discourage you from watching my travel vlogs or any other casual content. However, if there is a video on preparation strategy, then you can consider watching it if you think it helps you progress towards your ultimate goal. At all times, avoid other suggestions offered by YouTube that may end up distracting you.

You become smarter by consuming what is smart. And for me, smart content is whatever helps me achieve my long-term goal. Curate your social media and content consumption keeping this in mind.

~

Returning to the larger topic of 'Who is CA really for?', there's another misconception that only students who had Commerce in school should opt for CA. Let me narrate an interesting case of my friend, Parshva Dugad. He was studying Science in school and he wanted to pursue engineering after 12th. He studied hard and got into BITS Pilani. He was excited but something seemed amiss. He had packed his bags and was ready to move, but suddenly, a night before he was to leave, he unpacked his stuff and chose not to go. And the very next day he enrolled himself in CPT coaching. Just like you, all of us were left shocked. What suddenly changed in one night?

Turns out, for some time, he had been casually researching about careers in Finance and that led him to the CA curriculum. He got interested and researched more deeply, and his fascination for it grew further. He was aware that he wasn't from a Commerce background and that pursuing CA meant learning everything from scratch, including the basics taught in Class 11. The challenges of coping with the CA curriculum would come after that. What worked for him was that he made an infomed decision, from a position of awareness and with a belief in himself. Not only did he clear his CPT, he is also now a qualified Chartered Accountant.

Here's the thing. It's a myth that you must be from

Commerce background to do CA. As Parshva and so many others have shown, you can crack it even after studying Science, provided you're fully aware of what you'll be needed to do. Secondly and more importantly, all of this boils down to one thing: your mindset. If you have the correct mindset and an eagerness to learn, nothing can stop you. Even though my dad doesn't have the degree in CA that he yearned for, he still created a successful business because of his growth mindset.

Enroll for CA if you are interested in Finance and numbers, and have the patience, discipline, and consistency to sustain for 5 years of your life.

Don't enroll just because your parents pressurized you into it. It's not a course that someone could pass without one's own intrinsic dedication.

Also, don't enroll because of FOMO! Just because your best friend wants to do this doesn't mean it's automatically suitable for you too.

Undoubtedly, the course is tough and challenging. But that's also the reason it's enjoyable. After all, what's the point of succeeding at something easy? When I look back, despite and because of the challenges, I think those 5 years were truly the best of my life.

Don't let your limitations challenge you! Instead, challenge your limitations!

4. CPT - The First Step

The Common Proficiency Test (CPT), as you know, is the entry-level examination for admission to the Chartered Accountancy Course. It is similar to the "fastest-finger question" of KBC. Those who qualify sit in the hot seat of CA.

From 2020, the paper has changed, but when I took it, it comprised 200 multiple-choice questions (MCQs). Each correct answer fetched you 1 mark, and each incorrect answer was worth -0.25 marks. The questions were asked from 4 subjects: Fundamentals of Accounting, Mercantile Laws, General Economics, and Quantitative Aptitude.

To pass the exam, one must score a minimum of 50%

in all 4 subjects, which also meant at least a total of 100 out of 200 marks. CPT used to take place twice a year, on a Sunday in June and December.

Being in IGCSE has its perks and drawbacks. I won't call it a drawback per se but it ran on a different timeline than other curriculums like CBSE and ISC. Unlike students from these curricula, I was graduating from high school in November instead of March or April. So if I wanted to give CPT in December, I was left with only a month for preparation. But an important perk of IGCSE was that I was already abreast with half of the syllabus.

A month was still too less to prepare. So my first challenge in clearing CPT was the dilemma of when to appear for this exam.

So, early in 2015, my home was enveloped in a tense atmosphere. I was thoroughly confused. On a Sunday afternoon, my dad sat me down to discuss this conundrum. He insisted that I should appear for this exam in December itself. He reasoned that I was already aware of half the syllabus and if anything, I could reappear in June 2016 and this attempt could act as a dress rehearsal. I didn't say this out loud but since the beginning, I wanted to clear CA in a single attempt. Although I knew that even if I didn't do it, it would have been fine but call it my fallacy if you may. The question I asked myself was: Do I trust myself enough to appear for the exam in December and pass or should I wait till June 2016? I gave in to my dad's insistence and took the leap of faith. I decided to appear for the exam in December.

There is a quote by Sandeep Maheshwari that has been long embedded in my mind - "Don't think about the destination! Think about the way to reach the destination!" Now that I had the destination in my mind - clearing CPT on the first attempt - I started planning my roadmap to reach it. There wasn't time for even self-doubt and panic attacks. I joined my coaching for CPT in May 2015. For the next two months, my schedule was - school from 8 am to 3 pm, coming back for a quick lunch, then CPT coaching from 4-6.30 pm.

In the previous chapter, I discussed time prioritization. Let me now demonstrate how I applied it. I could have easily focused more on the CPT exam and settled for an average performance in my 12th boards, and eventually, it may not have made any difference to my goal. However, my dad's words kept ringing in my head like a mantra: "Find a balance. Anything in extreme is bad!" This voice refused to let me settle for average in my 12th boards. It encouraged me to give equal attention to both my board exams and CPT exam.

From July to November, I prioritized my 12th board exams and studied hard. On November 13th, 2015, I took a deep sigh of relief as I finished my last paper. After a good night's sleep, I woke up the next day with renewed vigour and began preparing for CPT, with only a month left.

In the following section, I will share how I prepared for my CPT exams.

Preparation Approach

I cannot guarantee that my preparation strategy will work for everyone, as we all have different ways of learning. But analyze for yourself and adopt whatever works best for you.

The golden mantra for my preparation throughout my CA journey is doing 3 readings of the syllabus. I never compromised on it.

So did I do all the 3 readings in a single month?! No. And what do these 3 readings look like? Let me explain properly.

- First Reading: Familiarize yourself with concepts and understand your syllabus deeply. Become friends with it.
- Second Reading: After making friends with the syllabus, dive deep into it. Highlight the important parts. E.g., I used to write 'R' above the important sections which I needed to revise just before my exams.
- Third Reading: Revision of the entire syllabus with

special focus on the highlighted sections.

I finished my first reading along with my coaching which took me two months. I finished my second reading in the 22 days from 13th November (my last board exam), and the third reading was done in the last 8 days before the CPT exam.

Apart from these 3 readings, I went through all the material provided by ICAI. I recommend all CA aspirants to treat the ICAI material like the Bible. I started solving the ICAI modules one month before my exam and it proved to be immensely helpful. In addition to the ICAI modules, I also referred to books by PC Tulsian.

I also had a strict strategy of writing at least two mock papers before the final exam. If time permits, you can write more, but two mock papers are the bare minimum. Doing two mock papers gives you an idea of how much you know and can score in the real paper, as well as how to manage time among the 200 questions.

Defying popular and safe advice, I went into my CPT exam with the goal of solving all 200 questions. Although I was aware of the 0.25 negative marking for each incorrect answer, I was confident in my ability to make up for it. Numbers have always made sense to me, so let's look at the math. Going strictly by probability, even if a chimpanzee took this exam, it would get 1 out of 4 questions right on average and still gain 0.25 marks. I considered myself smarter than a chimpanzee. This approach is tricky, however, and requires mastery of time management. If I can't solve a question, I should move on and not take it personally, as I could miss out on other questions and end up worse off.

After the Exam

After taking my CPT exam, I could finally relax. I was both calm and anxious while I waited for the results. I had done my best and now it was out of my hands. I had nothing left to do but wait with bated breath. We didn't know when the results would be announced until 13th January.

On this date, a notice came that the results would be out on the 16th January - in 3 days! I have a strange ritual of not telling my parents when the results are due. So, while I was anxious with anticipation on the result day, they were clueless. I told them the results would be out on 18th so that if I failed, I would have two days to process the information and find a way to tell them. But if I passed, I could surprise them immediately.

It was 1:30 pm on 16th. A friend called breaking the news. I went to the site on which the result was to come, but guess what happened? Yes, the site crashed.

After a tortuous wait of fifteen minutes and twenty

refreshes, the site finally came back on. I put in my details and my result sheet opened.

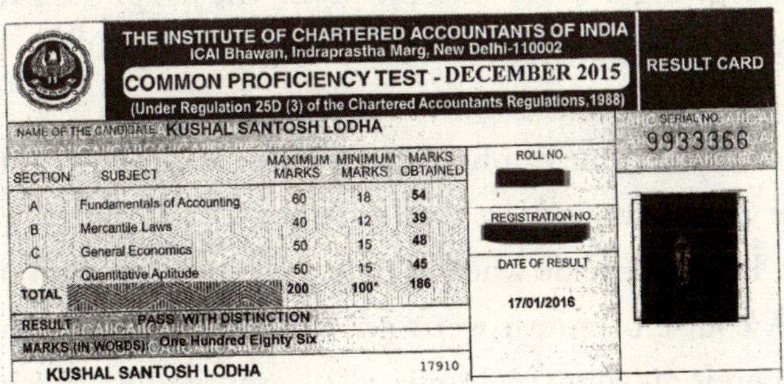

THE INSTITUTE OF CHARTERED ACCOUNTANTS OF INDIA
ICAI Bhawan, Indraprastha Marg, New Delhi-110002
COMMON PROFICIENCY TEST - DECEMBER 2015
(Under Regulation 25D (3) of the Chartered Accountants Regulations,1988)

RESULT CARD

NAME OF THE CANDIDATE KUSHAL SANTOSH LODHA

SERIAL NO. 9933366

SECTION	SUBJECT	MAXIMUM MARKS	MINIMUM MARKS	MARKS OBTAINED
A	Fundamentals of Accounting	60	18	54
B	Mercantile Laws	40	12	39
C	General Economics	50	15	48
	Quantitative Aptitude	50	15	45
TOTAL		200	100*	186

ROLL NO.

REGISTRATION NO.

DATE OF RESULT 17/01/2016

RESULT PASS WITH DISTINCTION

MARKS (IN WORDS) One Hundred Eighty Six

KUSHAL SANTOSH LODHA 17910

When I saw my result, I was unsure how to react. I went into the kitchen, where my family was talking, and just uttered, "186". All three of them looked at me, confusion on their faces.

My dad asked, "What do you mean?" I told them I had scored 186 out of 200 on my CPT.

As soon as I finished, my sister screamed with joy. My parents hugged me and were overjoyed. We called our relatives and shared the news with them.

In my time, the rank system had been abolished, so I was unsure of my standing in India. However, my tuition teacher was able to find it out through his inside sources. He told me that I had secured AIR 6 with my marks, and that was when I felt my first wave of happiness. It was then that I realised I had done it, and I was on my way to becoming a Chartered Accountant.

In Nashik, a hoarding was put up with my photo. For the next few days, our phone was ringing non-stop. I was giving interviews to the press. The happiness I felt was indescribable; it was something that could only be experienced.

Not everyone can be a rank holder, but even passing the CPT exam is more than enough. CPT is only a way for ICAI to decide whether to let you continue with the CA course or not; it won't get you an articleship. That depends on your CA Intermediate exam results. Passing CPT is just the first step.

But what if you failed?

One of the best pieces of advice I have ever received is: "Never let success go to your head, or else you will develop an ego. Instead, take it to your heart, celebrate it like a child who has been given an ice cream, and move on. In the event of failure, don't take it to heart, or else you will keep complaining. Instead, take it to your mind, analyze what went wrong, and try to improve to avoid making the same mistake again!"

In both cases, whether successful or not, you must keep going. If successful, strive for even greater accomplishments. If unsuccessful, move on and don't dwell on it; strive to keep improving.

Everyone experiences difficult times in life: financial struggles, failed exams, job rejections, health issues, and so much more. It's how we handle these challenges that matters. Realizing you're not alone in your struggles is essential.

On failure, I'd also suggest going back to the advice given in the previous chapter. Do you still satisfy the pre-requisite of your interest in finance? Are you still willing to be patient, disciplined, and consistent? Do you still have the desire to succeed? If the answer to all these continues to be yes, then learn from your mistakes, analyze what went wrong, and give your best in the next attempt. I repeat: it does not matter if you failed CPT in the first attempt.

If you have succeeded, congratulations! But don't lose yourself in celebrations. You need to now gear up for the second bigger storm: IPCC!

Today I'll do what others won't! So, tomorrow, I can do what others can't!

5. IPCC - The Second Storm

After passing the entrance test for CA, I prepared for the next challenge: the Integrated Professional Competency Course (IPCC). I decided to take a break in January before starting my coaching in February. Contrary to popular advice, I suggest taking a 15-day or one-month break before starting the preparation for IPCC. We all feel exhausted after the Foundation exam, so we need to give our minds time to recharge for the upcoming nine months. Listen to your body and take care of its needs.

After the break, I joined a coaching called Mind Spark Academy in Nashik in February. I have been asked a lot of questions about coaching. I have answered two of the most burning ones here.

Which mode of coaching should one opt for - online or offline?

Honestly, this depends on the kind of person you are. I've mentioned my understanding of what works and what doesn't for each.

Online:

This is suitable for someone who likes to study in the peace and comfort of their room. But one must be confident of staying diligent and not let procrastination derail the preparation.

The biggest drawback of recorded lectures is that procrastinating even one lecture often begins the spiral for more delays and they invariably pile up with time, and you're suddenly faced with a mountain to climb.

Also, students taking online classes should ensure their doubts are addressed periodically by their instructors. I have seen cases where instructors make grand promises at the start, but fail to follow through with helping students with their doubts. Make sure this doesn't happen to you.

Offline:

This is suitable for people who learn better in a classroom environment and have lots of doubts which they want to be addressed immediately. Also, if you think that you will end up procrastinating and need an external stimulus to keep you on track, opt for offline coaching.

On to the next question.

Which subjects should we join the coaching for?

My advice: Go through the entire syllabus of CA Intermediate and analyze which subjects you can study on your own. I attended coaching for all the subjects, but three months before the exam, I realized that I didn't need coaching for Audit and Law.

You should take this decision based on your memory capacity and how well you can understand the concept by yourself. Generally, you need to make this decision for theoretical subjects. For practical subjects, joining a coaching class would be a wise choice because it will get you to solve many questions in the class itself. And if you have any doubts, you can get them cleared immediately.

The right chronological order for attending coaching should be:

Practical subjects > Theoretical subjects > Taxation

I suggest ending your coaching with Taxation so that all the amendments that happen in the taxation laws are fresh in your mind.

No matter how many subjects you're taking coaching for, make sure you finish your classes three months before your exam. Use the last three months for self-study. I attended coaching from February to July, and then did self-study from August to October.

For those five months of my coaching, my schedule consisted of going to coaching from 8 am to 4 pm, returning home, and then playing a sport in the evening. I used to revise what had been taught to me in class, particularly for important subjects or for subjects in which I was weak.

However, I learned from my mistakes and suggest that you don't just revise for important subjects that you are weak in. Instead, revise all the things that you have been taught that day in your classes. Doing so will help you tremendously.

Preparation Approach

Contrary to popular belief, becoming a Chartered Accountant does not require sacrificing everything. In December 2022, I had the opportunity to be a panelist at the WICASA Surat mega-conference for CA students. While backstage, I spoke with Mr. Jay Chhaira, former Central Council Member of ICAI, who said that while CA is undoubtedly a tough degree, treating it like a monster will only make it more difficult. He suggested that students should learn to balance their studies with other activities. Dance while doing CA, sing while doing CA, play sport while doing CA, and above all, live while doing CA. I agree with him. Prioritizing is key. For five months, I volunteered with an NGO while also studying for the exam. Three months before the exam, however, I cut out all distractions. I switched off my phone and locked it in my dad's drawer. For those three months, I studied for twelve hours a day and locked myself in a room.

As I mentioned in the last chapter, time management is a myth, time prioritization is the key!

When I say I studied for twelve hours, I was careful to ensure that the time I put in was of high quality, not just a large quantity. I planned in such a manner that I never studied for four hours at a stretch. I believe in setting short-term goals and achieving them. So I had divided my day into six two-hour slots effectively.

I used to go to bed at 10 pm and wake up at 5 am precisely. I managed to study effectively by giving my mind proper breaks and ensuring I got seven hours of sleep to feel refreshed. Additionally, research has shown that our brains can only focus for 45 minutes at a time, so I would take a 5-minute break after each 45-minute session.

Similar to how I prepared for CPT, I followed the same golden mantra of 3 readings for IPCC too. I completed my first reading during the five months of coaching classes. My second reading took place in August and September 2016.

I completed my second reading for both groups in

August. For the first fifteen days (from August 1 to 15), I studied two subjects: one practical and one theoretical. In the mornings, I focused on the theoretical subjects, and in the afternoons, I studied the practical ones, as I'd often get sleepy after lunch. Theoretical subjects would have only aided me to sleep better. I finished Accounting and Law during this period. This is what I did:

Accounting:

- Practice manual and the study material from my notes and coaching
- To gain more confidence, I ordered a reference book called 'Padhuka' and solved all the numericals
- Took 3 RTPs and 2 MTPs

Law:

- Went through the entire study material
- Solved all the questions from the reference book by Munish Bhandari.
- Took 2 MTPs
- Note:
  - The reference book included past years' question papers and therefore, I did not separately do the RTPs.
  - I didn't refer to the practice manual as it was very detailed.
  - My friends from my senior batch advised solving

all the illustrations between the modules as questions were asked from there.

From 17th to 31st August, I did Costing and Tax. Here's my preparation summary for this phase:

Costing and FM:

- Went through the entire study material and practice manual
- Took 3 RTPs and 2 MTPs
- For theory, remembered the keywords and understood them in my own words.
- Note: My senior friends advised solving FM first, then attempting Economics. This is because after solving practical questions, you can decide how much time you have left for answering Economics questions and accordingly answer them in detail or concisely. Moreover, for Economics, they advised to practice lots of graphs and also from the 12th-grade Economics test book.

Tax:

- **Direct Tax:** The modules were extensive, so I studied from the reference book by Shri TN Manoharan, my favorite author. Little did I know that I would become so close to him later on and have the honour of attending his book launch of 'The Tech Phoenix' in Mumbai.

- **Indirect Tax:** ICAI Modules

Similarly, from 1st to 16th September, I did Advanced Accounting and Audit.

Advanced Accounting:

- Study material and practice manual
- Reference book - Padhuka

Auditing:

- Practice manual and Compiler

From 17th to 30th September, I completed IT and SM.

IT and SM:

- Practice manual and Compiler

I cannot emphasize this enough: treat ICAI material like the Bible. To this day, I regret not studying the internal reconstruction question from the study material that eventually appeared in Accounting Paper 1 which I goofed up.

Now that I was done with my second reading for both the groups in August and September, in October I revised both groups. I gave four days to each subject.

My golden rule for revising is to work backwards, which I also call the 'Reverse Order' strategy. Start by revising the last paper, then the paper before that, and so on. This approach ensures that the last few days of revision are in line with the first exam. I used to read all the highlighted parts in three days, and on the fourth day, I wrote either a mock test paper or a revision test paper for that subject.

The Exams and After

After three months of rigorous study, it was exam time. For some reason, I wasn't stressed at all during my exams. Maybe because I was confident with the preparation I had done.

My mindset for all papers was simple - try attempting 100 marks in each subject. Although I was clear about my approach and exam strategy, I did slip once.

I spent fifteen minutes solving a 4-mark question on one of my papers. My calculations showed that I had spent 7.8 minutes more than necessary. This caused me to panic, and I rushed through the rest of the paper. Unfortunately, I could not solve a question, and my goal of attempting the entire paper was not achieved.

The lesson I learned from this experience was to remain calm and confident during an exam. Panicking will only lead to mistakes.

Just remember: It'll all be okay in the end. If it's not okay, it's not the end!

After taking my exam, I had two to three months

until the results were announced. During that time, I took a week-long vacation to come out of my hibernation and become socially active again. I met up with friends and spent the first fifteen days relaxing. After settling in, I shifted my focus to developing my extra-curricular activities and soft skills that interested me and would be beneficial in the future.

I often get asked - "What extracurricular activities would look good on my CV?" My advice is to do what you enjoy learning and could also help you in the future of your chosen career.

In an episode of Konversation with Kushal, my friend Raj Shamani said something that sums up this question perfectly: our society has a result-oriented approach, but the result is only temporary. What matters is the process. Therefore, your motive shouldn't be to make your CV look good but to do what will make you happy. Adding soft skills to your CV is just a bonus. You should engage in these activities out of instinct.

I have a passion for public speaking and participated in many debate tournaments. I also enjoyed elocution. I hosted and moderated various events. To further my knowledge, I took online courses such as financial modeling from Udemy and classes on PowerPoint and MS Excel from Coursera.

I enjoy networking and meeting new people, so I

always make sure to attend the CA student conference. Sometimes I go as an attendee and other times as an anchor. To make my presence known, I ask questions to the panelists or present papers.

If you attend such conferences, I have a simple piece of advice: just ask questions! And don't fear being judged by others. Earlier on, I had this constant fear of what others would think if I asked a silly question. Conquer this fear. What do you think will actually happen even if you ask something silly? NOTHING! People will forget after the event or in a few days max. However, the guilt of not asking that question will always remain with you.

If you don't ask, the answer is always NO!

These conferences are an ideal way to foster relationships with more experienced people and expand your network. The ICAI used to host knowledge sessions and workshops, which I attended.

Among other things, I volunteered with NGOs, not for my CV's sake, but to actually give back to society. I kept up to date with current affairs by listening to podcasts like "All You Need to Know" by Bloomberg Quint. I also developed the habit of reading newspapers, such as the Economic Times, during this period.

I'm often asked - how do we get the information about events to attend? If you have the right network, information about upcoming events can be found easily.

They even float on WhatsApp chats. However, even if you don't have the network, you can still see the information on the ICAI website. On the website, go to the '**Announcements**' tab in the '**Students**' section to view all upcoming events with their details. You can apply to be a paper presenter or moderator directly on the website.

ICAI not only conducts knowledge workshops and sessions but also organizes fun activities such as cricket tournaments and trekking. There are plenty of opportunities available, such as the Center of Excellence Course by ICAI, it all boils down to how much you are willing to learn. You can also get information about upcoming events on social media by following their Instagram or LinkedIn handles.

Results

I spent the 2-3 months before the IPCC results developing the practical aspects of my life. Time flew quickly and, before I knew it, the results were set to be announced on January 31, 2017.

Unlike the previous time, my dad had found out the date of the results with his friend. But I was a step ahead still. While he knew of the date of the results, he wasn't aware of the time that they would be declared. I told them that the results were to be out in the evening around 5 pm but they came out in the morning itself. And as you'd expect, the site crashed again. I couldn't check my result. My friend offered to check it for me again and I denied him again.

Fifteen minutes passed with me refreshing and restarting my laptop several times before I could finally see my results. I saw the numbers 313 and 212, and FIVE HUNDRED TWENTY FIVE stated clearly.

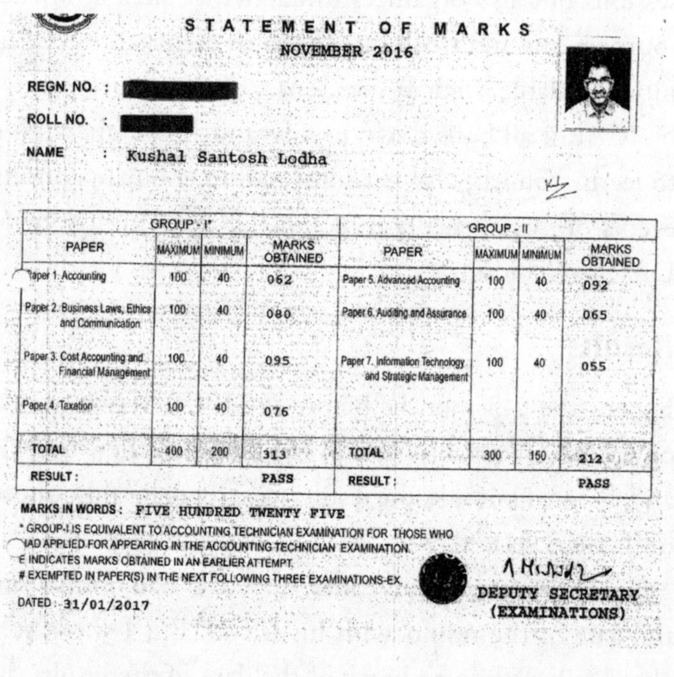

STATEMENT OF MARKS
NOVEMBER 2016

REGN. NO. :
ROLL NO. :
NAME : Kushal Santosh Lodha

GROUP - I*				GROUP - II			
PAPER	MAXIMUM	MINIMUM	MARKS OBTAINED	PAPER	MAXIMUM	MINIMUM	MARKS OBTAINED
Paper 1. Accounting	100	40	062	Paper 5. Advanced Accounting	100	40	092
Paper 2. Business Laws, Ethics and Communication	100	40	080	Paper 6. Auditing and Assurance	100	40	065
Paper 3. Cost Accounting and Financial Management	100	40	095	Paper 7. Information Technology and Strategic Management	100	40	055
Paper 4. Taxation	100	40	076				
TOTAL	400	200	313	TOTAL	300	150	212
RESULT :			PASS	RESULT :			PASS

MARKS IN WORDS : FIVE HUNDRED TWENTY FIVE

* GROUP-I IS EQUIVALENT TO ACCOUNTING TECHNICIAN EXAMINATION FOR THOSE WHO HAD APPLIED FOR APPEARING IN THE ACCOUNTING TECHNICIAN EXAMINATION.
E INDICATES MARKS OBTAINED IN AN EARLIER ATTEMPT.
EXEMPTED IN PAPER(S) IN THE NEXT FOLLOWING THREE EXAMINATIONS-EX.

DATED : 31/01/2017

DEPUTY SECRETARY
(EXAMINATIONS)

My IPCC Scorecard

It was a good score, of course. I secured AIR 10. My

family was ecstatic. Me? I was happy but not jubilant. Please don't judge me haha! I had scored 62 in Accounting whereas I was expecting at least 80.

The city of Nashik had never before seen an AIR 10 in the IPCC CA exam. News channels called, and I was featured on hoardings. I shared my marks with my tuition teacher, Mayur Sanghavi sir, who was the head of Mind Spark Academy. He was the first one to share my displeasure and expressed his disbelief that I had scored only 62 in Accounts. He asked me to send my paper for re-evaluation, but I was skeptical. In the past, re-evaluation had resulted in marks being deducted, which could have affected my rank and deprived me of the benefits the Top 10 rank holders were eligible to receive.

What were the benefits? My fee for CA final coaching was waived, I was eligible for the Center of Excellence Program in Hyderabad which usually cost around Rs. 48,000 which was waived for me, and ICAI awarded me a scholarship of Rs. 2,000/- per month. Although Rs. 2,000 per month might not seem like a huge amount, it meant the world to me as I had earned it on my own merit.

Re-evaluation was a gamble. Mayur sir called my dad and my dad sent my paper for re-evaluation. It took them four months to re-check my paper. During that time, the uncertainty of the re-evaluation result was overwhelming. Time is the most elastic element in the world; it slows down when we wait and speeds up when we enjoy.

After four long months, I was finally relieved and delighted to see my marks rise to 541/700. It turns out that the examiner had overlooked a 16-mark question. ICAI held a meeting to discuss my case and sent me the minutes. My rank was now 5 across India and I was ecstatic. They updated my rank with a pen on the printed sheet. That feeling is indescribable; it can only be felt. To this day, I am grateful to Mayur Sir for having such unwavering faith in me.

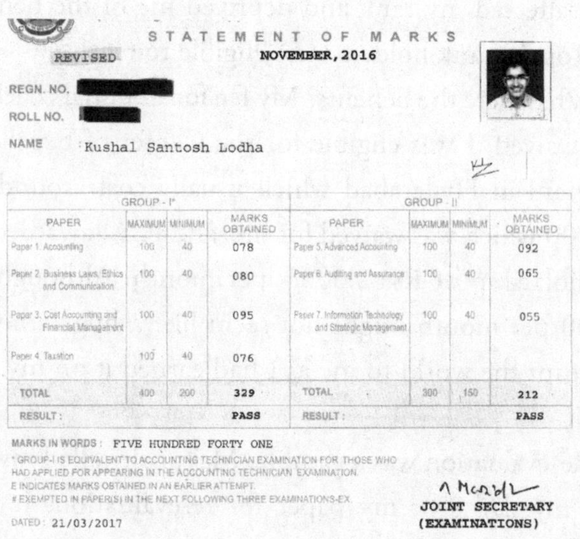

STATEMENT OF MARKS

REVISED

NOVEMBER, 2016

REGN. NO.

ROLL NO.

NAME : Kushal Santosh Lodha

GROUP - I*				GROUP - II			
PAPER	MAXIMUM	MINIMUM	MARKS OBTAINED	PAPER	MAXIMUM	MINIMUM	MARKS OBTAINED
Paper 1. Accounting	100	40	078	Paper 5. Advanced Accounting	100	40	092
Paper 2. Business Laws, Ethics and Communication	100	40	080	Paper 6. Auditing and Assurance	100	40	065
Paper 3. Cost Accounting and Financial Management	100	40	095	Paper 7. Information Technology and Strategic Management	100	40	055
Paper 4. Taxation	100	40	076				
TOTAL	400	200	329	TOTAL	300	150	212
RESULT :			PASS	RESULT :			PASS

MARKS IN WORDS : FIVE HUNDRED FORTY ONE

* GROUP-I IS EQUIVALENT TO ACCOUNTING TECHNICIAN EXAMINATION FOR THOSE WHO HAD APPLIED FOR APPEARING IN THE ACCOUNTING TECHNICIAN EXAMINATION.

E INDICATES MARKS OBTAINED IN AN EARLIER ATTEMPT.

EXEMPTED IN PAPER(S) IN THE NEXT FOLLOWING THREE EXAMINATIONS-EX

DATED : 21/03/2017

JOINT SECRETARY
(EXAMINATIONS)

My Updated IPCC Scorecard

There are additional benefits if you get a rank in the top 50.

The chances of securing an articleship with one of the Big 4 firms become significantly higher.

It may be a difficult reality to accept, but you will receive special attention from teachers during your coaching sessions. They will ensure that you comprehend the concepts and that all your queries are answered.

Moreover, your IPCC rank can get you a job in an MNC. A friend of mine got a job at BCG based on her rank in the CA Intermediate, not the CA Finals. If you want to get into industrial training, getting a rank will increase your chances of being accepted.

Are you at a disadvantage if you don't get a rank? Not necessarily. You just need to put in extra effort to ensure your academic and co-curricular records are good. You can still get an articleship in one of the Big 4 firms with a strong CV. But also make sure to get the best coaching for your CA Finals exams.

What if you don't qualify the IPCC? First advice: Don't give up! Take this setback as an opportunity to reflect on what went wrong and put in the effort to improve. In Malcolm Gladwell's book *Outliers*, he explains that if you put in 10,000 hours of practice, you can become an expert in that field. So, put in the work and become an expert in the subject. Remember, failing the IPCC doesn't mean the end of the world. Keep that in mind.

After passing your Intermediate exams, your real life is about to begin. You will enter a world full of politics, exposure, opportunities, and sometimes danger. You're about to get a taste of the real world. You will experience pain at times, and will feel like quitting, but remember:

Your purpose should be more powerful than the pain you are suffering!

6. Articleship - A Taste of the Real World

If someone were to ask me what the one thing I loved most about my CA journey was, I would say it was the three years of articleship. Articleship is a practical training program mandated by the ICAI that follows the IPCC exam. It gives you the opportunity to experience the real world at a very young age, as well as teaches you how to balance your personal and professional life while studying for the CA Finals.

My articleship began on April 1, 2017. For the first time, I left the comfort of my home and moved to Mumbai. I joined a mid-sized firm called Gokhale and Sathe in Mahim, Mumbai.

You may be wondering why, with an AIR 5 in IPCC,

I chose to join a mid-size firm instead of a BIG 4. What factors should determine which type of firm to join for articleship?

BIG 4 or not?

When deciding whether to join a mid-sized firm or a BIG 4, ask yourself what you see yourself doing in the future. If you envision yourself in a multinational corporation as a CEO or CFO, then BIG 4 is the best choice. However, if you plan to start your own practice or continue with a family practice, a mid-sized firm is more suitable.

To help you make an informed decision, I have listed the pros and cons of both BIG 4 and mid-sized firms on the following page.

As a thumb rule, note this carefully. If you wish to:

- Start your own practice —> join a mid-sized firm for articleship.
- Get a job in BIG 4 —> try your best to get into a BIG 4 for articleship.
- Get a job in an MNC or a corporate —> do industrial training.

If you are still unsure, don't worry. Explore all the possible options. If you're a CA, you're the jack of all and master of one, you can switch fields.

Big 4:

Pros	Cons
• **Exposure to corporate life:** An articleship at a BIG 4 would expose you to corporate life very early. With opportunities to work with both domestic and international clientele, you'd be better groomed by the time you finish with better soft skills.	• **Work may be narrow and filtered:** Unlike in a mid-sized firm, in a BIG 4 due to hierarchical structure, you will likely get exposed to only some facets of work and not the entire spectrum of work that can be undertaken by a CA. You won't work directly under the partners.
• **Better shortlisting chance during placements:** A BIG 4 tag adds tremendously to your CV and makes you desirable for MNC jobs later on. BIG 4 articleship often leads to more shortlists during final placements.	• **Only single department exposure:** In a BIG 4, there is no rotational policy. You will have exposure to one department only. It's good if you're looking to specialize in that work, but not good if you see yourself as a more generalist finance person.
• **Conversion into full-time role**: Many times, BIG 4 offer a permanent job based on good articleship performance	• **Long hours during peak season:** During peak season you might have to work late, sometimes even till midnight, and that might hamper

Mid-size Firm:

Pros	Cons
• **All-round exposure**: In mid-sized firms, there is a rotational policy where every 6 months, you're moved to a different department. You get to explore more and better understand the profile you like most.	• **No Brand**: The brand value is nowhere compared to a BIG 4. There are a lot of mid-size firms in India but only four BIG 4!
• **Lesser working hours**: The number of working hours is usually lesser than a BIG 4. This leaves you with more time to focus on your studies as well as extracurricular activities.	• **Lower MNC shortlists**: Many MNCs only shortlist candidates with BIG 4 articleship experience. Their perception is that a BIG 4 articleship prepares one better for the corporate life and the candidate is more ready to be absorbed in their organization.
• **No hierarchy**: Lack of hierarchy in a mid-sized firm means you get to work directly with partners and managers. This helps you understand how to run a firm and learn directly from them, which is not possible at a BIG 4.	• **No exposure to international clientele**: This is self-explanatory. Mid-sized firms only cater to Indian clients so if you really wish to work in an international setting, you won't get it here.

The How and Where of Articleship

Let's answer some of the common questions students have about articleship.

"If I get into a mid-size firm, will I have to stay there for 3 years?"

This is a question I have been asked many times. The answer: **No.**

Transferring between firms is an option for those who don't enjoy their current job. If you're moving from a mid-sized firm to a Big 4, your CV should be outstanding and you must have a strong letter of recommendation. To get the best of both worlds, it's recommended to start with a Big 4 in the first year and then transfer to a mid-sized firm. However, transferring too frequently can make you appear unreliable, so it's best to avoid doing so.

What are the criteria to get into a BIG 4?

If you have a rank in CA Intermediate, you have a great opportunity to secure an articleship with one of the Big 4 firms. But what about those who don't have a rank? Can they still get an articleship with Big 4? Yes! You can still get an articleship with Big 4, but you'll need an exemplary CV for that.

What do I mean by an exemplary CV? It means that, in addition to having strong academic credentials, your extracurricular activities should also be impressive. This could include presenting a paper, moderating a paper presentation, volunteering at an NGO, and participating in student conferences.

How to apply at these BIG 4?

Having a strong network is always beneficial. If you don't have one, you can find the email address of the HR department on the company's website, under the "Careers" section, and send them your resume. You can also upload your resume there. Leverage social media, such as LinkedIn, to reach out to the HR personnel of the company you wish to get into. When sending a connection request, don't forget to include a note introducing yourself. Additionally, websites such as Fast Careers, iimjobs, cajobportal, and Phenom Placements can provide information about vacancies in these companies. The ICAI website also provides updates about vacancies, so check it regularly. Finally, there are CA WhatsApp groups where such messages are shared.

My Articleship Experience

By now you must have guessed why I did my articleship at a mid-sized firm. I wanted to go back to Nashik and start my practice. This is what I had thought back then but look what I am doing right now! So don't worry if your articleship doesn't go as per your 'plan'. Life will surprise you in different ways and you'll end up better for it.

3rd April 2017 - my first day at my firm. I was beyond nervous and emotional. In an instant, I was out of my comfort zone. For the first time in my life, I took a crowded local train instead of being driven in a car, where there is no concept of space. When I arrived at the office at 9:30 am, I was given an introductory session that improved my mood. I tried to stay positive and optimistic. But by the end of the day, my courage had shattered. I was welcomed to the real world with the strictest manager in the firm. Welcome to the real world - it's not what you expect. It sucks! Trust me, it SUCKS!

For the first seven months, I worked in the bank audit department with 3 articles and 1 partner. We had meetings twice a week, and in each one, the manager would blast us. I still remember an instance when I was scolded harshly for a minor mistake. It was a Saturday at 7:30 pm and I had finished my work. With trembling legs, I mustered the courage to ask for permission to leave, but my manager blasted me, asking how I could leave while they were still working?

I experienced another incident once when I went to a client's place. After completing my work ahead of schedule, I asked them to cover for me with my manager. I requested them to lie to my manager that my phone wasn't working and I had gone to get it fixed if she called. As luck would have it, my manager called the client's landline that day. When I reached my hostel, the clients called me to let me know. I was trembling when I called my manager to explain the situation.

Facing a difficult time at work and struggling to adjust to life in Mumbai, I had to travel to Vasai, a nearby town, for six months for work-related purposes. The round trip took three hours, and my company was reimbursing me only for auto rides. And I wasn't alone on these rides; there were four other passengers, not including the driver.

I was coming to terms with the fact that the childhood mantra of "study hard now and the rest of your life will be easy" was a lie. I had secured a rank in my CA Intermediate, yet here I was. I couldn't take it anymore, so I called home and told my dad I couldn't do it. He shouted at me and asked, "What is this brat behavior? It's normal to travel for three hours. Thousands of people travel in the same local and auto that you are traveling in. Do they complain? No. So learn to adjust."

In fact, let me share something that will blow your mind. One of these days when I was finding it tough to cope with the new life, I requested my dad, "Can I please come back to Nashik?"

"Why, what happened?", he asked.

"I am fed up with this articleship life and I can't work for anyone else. Can I please join your business and let us grow together?", I murmured.

He responded, "If you come back to Nashik, even I won't allow you to join the business. I don't want to work with people who quit easily. I want people who are adaptable to change, can learn to adjust, and can be tough at times." I was stunned.

There was no easy way out, not even into my dad's business! Although I was taken aback, the fact that nothing good comes without working hard for it was inculcated firmly after this incident.

~

But what hurts you can also bless you. Those seven months, when it felt like the world was against me, were some of the best of my life. They taught me how to adjust and be flexible. Without anyone to turn to for help, I had to rely on my own hard work. I searched on Google, listened to podcasts, and watched YouTube videos to clear my doubts. Being reprimanded for mistakes made me even more careful to be perfect.

After a seven-month stint, I was transferred to the GST Compliance and Advisory department for the next seven months. Having already endured the worst, nothing could compare. This stint was good.

I once traveled to Pune with my manager to fight a VAT case. I used the time while we were traveling to learn from him. While I learned directly from our conversations, I also learned indirectly how to make the most of my time. He was reading about GST the entire journey. This taught me to always make the most of my time and learn whenever I can.

My last assignment was in the Direct Taxation/ Assessment/Litigation department, and it was my best experience. I was given great exposure during the eighteen months I was there, and I was the only article to be given the opportunity to argue a case law. My manager was excellent and would resolve any doubts I had. I learned how to effectively argue my point.

But as much as we try, we all make mistakes. I was filing Form 15CA when my manager forwarded me an email from the client. In it, the client had written the entire address and at the end, added "keep blank". Without thinking, I copied and pasted the entire address into the form, including the "keep blank". When I showed my work to my manager, he started laughing. I was confused, so I asked him what was wrong. He pointed out my mistake and, instead of scolding me, he made me realize the importance of valuing junior employees through his demeanour. His name is Kedar Phadke and I am forever grateful for his teachings, which have shaped my personality. I have never had a better boss and if I ever wish for one in the future, I pray that I get someone like him!

He was kind enough to take me everywhere he went, so I accompanied him to the appellate court. The client was appealing against the Department of Income Tax. It was a great learning experience; I improved my communication skills by interacting with the Commissioner of Income Tax, and my drafting skills by drafting submissions and opinions for judges and the Commissioner. This learning also helped me in my studies for CA Final, as I was able to type and read case laws, making them easier to remember.

Articleship wasn't just about work; we had plenty of fun too. I took the initiative to organize office parties, and I'd like to encourage all of you to do the same. Companies want an all-rounder, not just a corporate drone.

One time, we had a Bollywood-themed party in my office. I dressed up as Circuit from Munna Bhai MBBS. What an evening it was!

Me as Circuit

Dummy Articleship - Should You Do It?

NEVER opt for a dummy articleship. That is sheer stupidity. People who opt for it argue that the extra time will help them prepare better for CA Final and score well in it. BULLSHIT! Most such students waste even their first year of articleship partying and horsing around. ICAI wants to teach you how to manage your time between academics and the real world, and a dummy articleship defeats that purpose.

Articleship provides practical knowledge and develops skills. It is essential for growth. I always emphasize that knowledge without practical application is useless and practical application without theoretical concepts is dangerous. I have witnessed many people who opted for dummy articleship fail their exams. The knowledge gained while working will eventually help you score better too.

For the first two weeks of my articleship, I was assigned vouching, verification and scrutiny tasks. All I had to do was match the invoice amount with that in the software. It was a tedious job, but it is the basics of accounting. If you understand this, then complex concepts will become easier.

Balancing Academics with Articleship

If you're working in a Big 4, chances are you will end up working for 10-12 hours a day or even more. I am sure you would be silently cursing your managers as they eat into your daily study hours or disallow you from going on study leave (unless you have a manager like mine :)).

To be honest, managing your academics with articleship is not that difficult. Ideally, try to revise what has been taught in the class on the same day. Let's say you come back from your office by 8 pm, give an hour, and revise all the concepts quickly on weekdays. However, fortunately or unfortunately, if you are in a Big 4 and have no time on weekdays, I would suggest making most of your weekends studying and revising what has been taught in the classes.

Worst case, if you're not even getting time on weekends, I suggest revising the entire subject immediately after the coaching is over by taking a short break post the assignment.

I'd definitely not recommend studying during office hours or taking books to the office to study when you find free time. Instead, use that time to learn more practical things and ensure you are extracting the most out of your articleship. Even if you study in your office, you will end up being disturbed by some other notorious article who will taunt you, "That person studies during office hours also. He/she never works." Bla bla bla! Moreover, concentrating in the office would anyway be difficult due to disturbances. Some people just study to show that they are studying regularly for CA Exams to create panic for others. Stay away from them!

Reflecting on My Learnings

During my three years, I learned the importance of balance. In my first year, I focused on gaining experience and exposure. For the next two years, I managed my studies and work. I would wake up at 6 am, attend coaching classes for CA Final from 7 to 10 am, and then work from 10:45 am to 7:45 pm. In the evenings, I'd play table tennis with my friends. I strived to be successful but also took out time to have fun. I attended meetings and went out partying. I was punctual at work, but sometimes I'd stay out late and break curfew. All in all, I found a balance between work and play.

The only thing I regret is not doing industrial training during my articleship. Industrial training, which is usually done in the last year of articleship, provides invaluable exposure to how a particular industry works. Undergoing it increases one's chances of getting shortlisted by MNCs significantly. Moreover, the company in which you do your training often offers a permanent job based on your performance, and the payment for a CA fresher is usually higher than in the BIG 4.

If you wish to pursue industrial training, you should begin studying for CA Finals from day 1, as the preparatory period becomes shorter. An ideal profile would be to achieve a rank while doing industrial training. However, remember this:

It is better to have a rank in CA Final without

industrial training than to have no rank in CA Final with industrial training.

Therefore, take your decision accordingly.

Well, what did my articleship days (2017–2020) teach me?

☞ **Punctuality:** Once, I arrived at my office at 10:02 am, but the client meeting was scheduled for 10:00 am. My manager was furious, as it was unprofessional to enter a client meeting after the client has already arrived. I realized I should make sure to arrive at least 15 minutes before any scheduled meeting.

☞ **Discipline:** I noticed one of my juniors had a strict routine: waking up at 4:45 am and studying in the library from 5 am until 9:45 pm, allowing for seven hours of sleep. Inspired by him, I decided to adopt the same routine. I was motivated to become more disciplined!

☞ **Multi-tasking:** I enjoyed taking part in extracurricular activities, but not at the expense of my academics. I made sure to give my articleship the attention it deserved, study for my classes, and volunteer or organize events to learn something new. This taught me how to multitask effectively. I'm a huge fan of multitasking, and if you automate some of the tasks, you can do it even better! Trust me!

☞ **Time Management:** Attending classes from 7 am and quickly heading to the office, then reviewing the material after returning home, forced me to manage my time effectively. It's not easy, especially when you're trying to figure out your life goals and are overwhelmed with work and school!

The articleship experience, when I did it, was certainly not easy. I was challenged and questioned on a daily basis, both at work and in daily life, but that's exactly what led to my growth. In the quest to overcome hurdles frequently, I became better at so many things without even realizing. Even though they were sometimes a pain in the ass, I wouldn't trade those three years for anything.

Move out of your comfort zone. Experience the pain of the real world. Focus on the positives rather than complaining about the negatives.

Growth is inversely proportional to the size of your comfort zone!

The more you stay in your comfort zone, the lesser your chances of growth.

During my articleship days

7. Hostel - A Finishing School for Life Skills

Moving out of my home to Mumbai for my articleship was a difficult decision. But, where would I live in Mumbai? My dad and I had different opinions on this. He wanted me to live in a hostel, while I wanted to move into a flat.

He asked me why I was so afraid of living in a hostel. I wanted to be independent and felt that a hostel would be too restrictive. After an hour, he finally convinced me to try a hostel for six months and if I didn't like it, I could switch to a flat.

What was his motive behind pushing me for the hostel? He wanted me to live in the company of other people and learn the art of networking and making connections. After an hour, I had no other option but to agree. So it was decided that I would move into a hostel and if I didn't like it after six months, I would switch to a flat.

~

RVG Educational Foundation in Andheri is renowned for its excellent hostel for CA students, catering to those of Marwari and Rajasthani backgrounds. If you thought CA was tough, try getting into this hostel! The admission process is two-fold: a merit list based on CA exam results, and an interview. The interview is often likened to a campus placement, as it involves questions such as why the hostel should accept you and what your future goals are. I was fortunate enough to gain admission to the hostel on merit, thanks to my rank in the IPCC exam.

I shifted in April 2017 to RVG. After getting through such a tedious process, I expected that hostel would be worth it. As soon as I entered, all my imagination was shattered. It was nothing like the fancy dorm rooms they show in shows and on TV but everything like the hostel shown in the movie *3 idiots*. There was no AC. I melted like a heap of salt standing in my room in the sultry air of April. During the summer months, cold showers became my only way to survive that weather without an AC.

Adjusting to a hostel initially was a challenge. Having been spoiled my whole life, I was now on my own. But the air conditioning was the least of my worries. Everyone has something they're scared of, and for me it was insects. Living in RVG meant I had to confront this fear. Our rooms were the breeding grounds for bedbugs. I used to sleep on a bedbug-infested bed, and they spread to my wardrobe too.

One day, I was working in my Partner's office with four articled assistants when I felt something moving on my arm. Suddenly, I saw a bedbug leisurely crawl out of my sleeves. I was so shocked. My colleagues saw it and immediately told me to throw it outside. When I returned, the first thing they asked me was if I lived in a jungle LOL! I was appalled.

This incident was the tipping point for my breakdown. Enough was enough. That evening I called my dad and declared I couldn't live here anymore. He comforted me and asked me to give this hostel another chance. What doesn't kill you, makes you stronger, he said. I still remember my tear-stained pillow that night. I cried silent tears as I didn't want to let my roommates in on my weak moment.

~

Moving to a hostel felt like my bubble of comfort had burst, and I had no choice but to grow. I had to overcome my hesitation in talking to strangers. During dinner, I started conversations with some of them and eventually they became my friends. I was surrounded by incredibly talented people: national-level guitarists, violinists, coders, and even a beatboxer. Seeing them, it felt like they were doing CA as a side job. We'd play cricket on weekends, party, and have jamming sessions at night.

According to a study conducted by Harvard anthropologist Joseph Henrich, human success is not due to individual intelligence, but rather our collective intelligence. Henrich's book, *The Secret of Our Success*, states: "Innovation in our species depends more on our sociality than on our intellect."

Living in a hostel with many smart people, I learned to take advantage of collective intelligence. Our late-night conversations were a great way to learn from each other. Harsh Nenawati, a friend of mine, was nicknamed the "Warren Buffett of RVG." He had been investing in the stock market since the age of 13 and knew it inside out.

He'd conduct in-depth research before investing in any stock. He would talk to people from the hostel and ask them questions about their work. For instance, if someone worked in the audit department, he would seek their opinion on the company's performance and future potential. He would analyze the data he collected and use it to make decisions about which stocks to invest in.

Through Harsh, I realized that we can achieve a lot if we stop wasting time.

My junior, Gaurav Sarawagi, taught me the importance of staying focused on long-term goals and avoiding short-term pleasures. Since the first day in the hostel, he would wake up at 4:45 am and study in the library from 5 am. He would go to bed at 9:45 pm to get 7 hours of sleep. He ended up getting AIR 1 in his CA Inter exams. I followed his example and tried waking up early to be in the library at 5 am. His dedication and discipline inspired me. I learned from him that if the people around you don't inspire you, it's not a circle, it's a cage. Luckily, mine was a circle and nothing like a cage. They motivated me to set high goals instead of getting stuck in comparison and jealousy.

~

During my hostel days, I learned what we Indians call *jugaad*. For example, on one particular night, we returned to the hostel after partying into the wee hours of the morning. To get in, we printed letters from our firm and forged signatures.

Although I'm not proud of it, we occasionally bribed the security guard to enter the premises past the curfew. We also sometimes skipped classes.

Once, four of my friends were suspended due to their involvement in a notorious birthday celebration for a guy in the hostel. What did the celebration look like? It was one of those occasions where your friends make you regret being born, as they thrash you with full-fledged kicks and beatings. For a week, these four had to fend for themselves. They managed to stay and feed themselves, as well as come up with ways to make up for their missed classes, as when you are suspended, you are not allowed inside the hostel campus.

Being resourceful (*jugaadu*) is extremely important, as following all the rules does not teach you problem-solving. The hostel was the place where we could do all the things that we had missed out on in college. In fact, the word *jugaad* has now been added to the Oxford dictionary with the definition - *"a flexible approach to problem-solving that uses limited resources in an innovative way."*

Everyone should live in a hostel at least once. Being on your own helps with personal growth and teaches valuable lessons. It also improves communication skills as you have to interact with strangers and make new friends. Teamwork is also developed through opportunities such as organizing the annual RVG fest, Aagaaz. I participated in the Mr. RVG event, even though I didn't have the physique. I confidently sang a rap on the stage: "*Jaise jeetne ke liye bana hai race ka ghoda, vaise Mr. RVG ke liye bana hai Kushal Lodha.*" LOL!

I put aside my fears of being judged and sang in front of the entire hostel. Although I didn't win and came in the second place, I gained the confidence to be unashamed in front of an audience. Apart from this, I also learned how to manage time and balance our commitments. We used to hold meetings for Aagaaz and work until 2-3 am with a bowl of Maggi, then go to our respective offices at 9 am. All of these opportunities are missed if you live in a flat.

With a simple Google search, you can find hostels for CAs in any city.

On the last day, we had tears in our eyes as were leaving the hostel, ready to move on to the next chapter in our lives. As I walked out, I internally thanked my dad for making the best decision for me. He was right; living in a hostel did change me for the better.

If there are two instances in my life where I have cried silently, it has to be the day when I joined my hostel and the day when I left my hostel!

8. The 'Final' Frontier

You are now just one step away from your dream to become a CA - CA Finals. This last fight is not going to be easy though. This is where most people encounter this villain called 'burnout'. But your job is not to burn 'out' but to simply burn and shine like the sun!

I don't mean to trivialize the actual burnout experienced by so many professionals and students around the world. But through this chapter, I'd want to help you develop routines and habits that will help you tide through this phase smoothly. Often, burnout is a consequence of inefficiency. As a CA student, you can't afford it, with so much volume of content to consume and comprehend.

Technically, you are given 3 years to prepare for CA Final. ICAI expects you to manage your preparation along with your articleship. But in the first year of my articleship, I didn't study much and preferred to gain as much practical experience as possible. I'd strongly suggest the same to everyone.

In the second year of my articleship, I joined the coaching for CA Final. My attempt was in November 2019 and I started these classes exactly 2 years before. Although I took coaching for all the subjects, I realized it was unnecessary in four of them.

Preparation Approach

Do revise the topics along with the classes. It will give you a massive edge during your five months of preparatory leave and your concepts would be reinforced even more. Like I have said previously, make sure to finish your coaching for all subjects at least five months before your attempt.

I went back to Nashik on 15th June 2019 to prepare for my CA Final. I had four and a half months for self-study before appearing for the exam. 4-5 months are enough to prepare for it. I have seen aspirants take 6-7 months of leave and still flunk, and also students who got ranks after just preparing diligently for 3-4 months. It all boils down to just one thing - your sincerity. And as if to test my sincerity towards my goal, fate too took a test of me.

The biggest sacrifice I made during my CA Finals journey was not contributing properly to my sister's wedding preparations. The exams were in November 2019 and the wedding was in the first week of July.

I also gave my CFA exam on 15th June, post which I tried studying for 12 hours a day for CA Finals but had a difficult time due to the buzz of the wedding season. After all, even I wanted to enjoy, right? Who would not?

I planned my day out so that I could take at least 2 hours a day to go to the dance practice and help in any small way possible. I ensured that I finished at least one subject in those 20 days as I knew I'd be fully involved in the wedding from 3rd to 8th July. Of course, I did not want to miss the main functions.

Immediately from the next day i.e. 9th July, I started studying with full concentration and ensured there was no distraction until the exams got over.

In fact, when my results were announced, my sister was the happiest and she mentioned, "It is because of your self-control and all those sacrifices which got you the rank in your exams!"

The point of this is that if you plan well, executing anything becomes simpler, however hard it may be. Making excuses and blaming external circumstances won't help you qualify. Plan your preparation so well that even an unplanned break of a week or two doesn't derail the outcome.

Plan and Execute. Don't Fail and Complain!

My preparation strategy for the CA Final didn't change much. Similar to my IPCC exam, I completed my first reading and highlighted the important things along with my coaching. I had finished coaching for all my subjects by June so the next four and half months were set aside for self-study. For those months, I had divided my day into six slots of two hours each with ample amounts of breaks in between. I used to take five minutes' break after every forty-five minutes.

Let me in you on a secret to keep away from distractions - I never watched anything entertaining in my break time. I once watched the movie *Rustom* during my IPCC and I got so engrossed that I kept thinking about the ending for the rest of the day. By night, I realized I had wasted an entire day. The next day, I asked my dad to cut the cable of TV. Also, I have not watched TV ever since. But I'm still happy. In fact, I am happier!

My point in recounting this experience is that if you watch anything or play any video game during your break, you will likely think about it subconsciously or consciously. During my break, I used to listen to motivational videos or spend time with my family. I remember I had downloaded some study instrumental music on my mom's phone, which I would play in my headphones while studying. Her phone was kept in the hall, in airplane mode. The music I listened to has this title on YouTube: *Evening Waves • Relaxing Piano Music with Ocean Waves.*

Distractions are not just limited to TV, internet, and video games, but extend to food as well. It's essential to stay physically healthy during preparation, and consuming junk will adversely impact your body. Once, my mom ordered a sandwich at home but I had abstained from eating any outside food for four months. I didn't want to get sick and affect my planning and deadlines. Despite my craving for my favourite sandwich from my favourite place in Nashik, I controlled myself. The more you practice self-control, the more you'll adapt and avoid bad habits.

I completed my first reading in my leave period till 30th September. Ideally, I would recommend dedicating 2 months each to group 1 and group 2. Till my CA Final, I had built the habit of studying two subjects per day - one theoretical and one practical. For my CA Final, I gave fifteen days per subject. This meant that I studied 6 hours of theory in the morning and 6 hours of a practical subject in the evening.

Deep in Study

Subject-wise Strategy

For group 1 my subject combinations were FR & Audit, and SFM & Law. I have illustrated my subject-wise strategy below:

FR:

- Modules and Class notes
- Previous year RTPs
- Note: Solve the RTPs, as they contain a variety of new questions and make up the majority of the question paper. Additionally, there will surely be one or two new questions.

SFM:

- For Theory: Modules with special attention to chap-

ters like Risk Management, Financial Policy, Corporate Strategy, Securitization, and Start-up Finance
- For Practical: Practice Manual of the old course with special attention to Forex, Derivatives, Mutual Funds, and so on.

Law:

- Reference book by Manish Bhandari
- For MCQs: Only ICAI material and sample questions
- Previous attempts RTPs and MTPs

Audit:

- All three modules and drone charts of Sarthak Jain
- Note: For Audit, one needs to thoroughly complete the practice manuals. In the paper, they ask direct questions from the module. I remember in my attempt they asked the difference between Schedule 3, Division II and Division III - a question not found in any reference book. Additionally, it is important to memorize all the bullet points given in the module, as they may ask questions based on them, as they did in my time when they asked "Elucidate the circumstances under which risk can arise or change."

In the next one and a half months, I completed Group 2. For Group 2, my subject combinations were

Costing & Direct Tax, Risk Management, and Indirect Tax. I have illustrated my subject-wise strategy below:

Costing:

- Modules
- If and only if you have the time, practice the manual of the old course. I didn't find it too effective.

Risk Management:

- Modules
- Read some company's risk reports
- All previous MTPs
- Case studies on the ICAI website
- Note: I made a thorough index in alphabetical order for Risk Management. It was a 600 rows' long document where I listed out all the important keywords.

Direct Taxation:

- Compact and Compiler by Bhanwar Borana Sir
- All 4 modules of ICAI
- Note: Important to read and memorize case laws. I wrote them on a piece of paper and used to revise them first thing in the morning.

Indirect Tax:

- All 4 Modules of ICAI
- Yashvant Mangal's book for solving questions
- Sample MCQs of ICAI

- 3 RTPs and 2 MTPs
- Note: Modules for the Indirect Tax are the best!

In October, I revised for both groups. Continuing with my ritual, I revised in the reverse order dedicating four days per subject. For three days, I would revise the subject and write a mock test paper on the fourth.

Staying Motivated

Just like every other aspirant, I felt burnt out during this phase. I went through a cycle of demotivation. Missing my sister's birthday party and only being able to wish her for fifteen minutes was taking its toll. But here's what kept me motivated: the placebo effect.

I simply explain this as "fooling your brain" and repeating to yourself "all is well". Whenever I felt discouraged, I reminded myself of why I started this journey, my dad's story, and my goal. I also watched motivational videos by Sandeep Maheshwari to keep me motivated. This helped me stay on track.

Check out my daily routine in the table given on the next page.

In his book *Outliers*, Malcolm Gladwell argues that everyone owes something to their parentage and patronage. In the last leg of the battle, I was able to score well due to my hard work, but also because of my patronage.

Time	Details	Study Hours
05:00 am to 05:30 am	Meditation	-
05:30 am to 08:00 am	Theoretical Subject	2.5
08:00 am to 08:15 am	Shower	-
08:15 am to 08:45 am	Breakfast 1	-
08:45 am to 10:45 am	Theoretical Subject	2
10:45 am to 11:30 am	Breakfast 2 and friends doubt solving	-
11:30 am to 01:30 pm	Theoretical Subject	2
01:30 pm to 02:00 pm	Lunch	-
02:00 pm to 04:00 pm	Practical Subject	2
04:00 pm to 04:30 pm	Temple (Darshan)	-
04:30 pm to 05:00 pm	Jogging Track	-
05:00 pm to 05:30 pm	Evening Snacks	-
05:30 pm to 07:30 pm	Practical Subject	2
07:30 pm to 08:00 pm	Dinner	-
08:00 pm to 09:30 pm	Practical Subject	1.5
09:30 pm to 10:00 pm	Friends doubt solving	-
10:00 pm to 05:00 am	Sleep	-
Total		12

My daily routine during Finals preparation

For four months, my maid cleaned my room - dusting, sweeping and mopping within fifteen minutes of my break time. Mangesh, the milkman, used to bring fresh milk every day at 7 am sharp. My parents stopped having guests over so I wouldn't be disturbed. Instead, they visited other people's houses.

Realizing I wasn't spending enough time with my family, I decided to rearrange my schedule and have meals with them. My dad would come for lunch at 1.30 pm sharp, no matter how important his meetings or work were.

I called my mentor, Mayur Sir, at 9.30 pm one night. He was in the middle of a wedding, yet he took out half an hour to solve all of my doubts, knowing I had a paper the next day. Another time, I called him at 5.30 am on the day of my paper to ask doubts. Even half asleep, he answered all my queries.

Every Sunday from 9.30 to 10 pm, I would call my friend and junior, Gaurav Sarawagi, to clear my doubts. Talking to him made me understand where I was lacking.

As you can see, there were so many factors involved in my success. A drop of water is worthless but zillions of drops make the ocean. These drops made my entire ocean of CA Journey. On top of that, I was also lucky that I stayed healthy throughout those four months, eating clean and rarely going out.

During Exams

After four and a half months of preparation, it was exam time. To make the most of the last days, let me share a final piece of preparation advice to conquer this 'final frontier'. For the preparatory leave, we discussed the preparation strategy in detail. The most crucial phase is one and a half-day break between each exam. It's essential to make the most of these one-and-a-half days. To do this, it's important to understand both - what to study and what not to.

In such a small gap, you can't revise the entire syllabus. You need to be smart. Revise all the topics you marked as important during your third reading, and the portions you find difficult. Don't spend time on topics you find easy.

My routine for these days looked something like this: after giving the exam, I took the day off and slept by 8.30 pm. I woke up the next day at 5 am, refreshed after a good night's sleep. I studied for 14 hours that day. On the day of the paper, I studied from 5 am to 1 pm, and the paper started at 2 pm.

~

Your hard work hinges on those 3 hours. Therefore, it's essential to remain calm and not panic. During the 15 minutes of reading time, don't worry about whether you can solve the questions; instead, number them according to your confidence in solving them.

After the writing time starts at 2 pm, solve the MCQs latest by 2.30 pm. This time too, I went with the approach of solving the entire paper. I allocated the time given to one question based on the marks it carries. For example, if the question is for 4 marks then 4 / 100 x 180 = 7.2 minutes. If you end up spending more time on a question, then make sure you pick up your pace in the next one. I carried a stopwatch with me to keep track of time.

I began with the question I was surest of. I made sure my answer sheet was neat and had minimal strike-throughs. I wrote concisely and highlighted the key-words. Presentation is important, as first impressions count. The examiner can form an opinion of you based on your answer sheet, so make sure it is of good quality. Remember the section numbers and use them in your answer sheet; this will show the examiner you have studied for the exam. You can view my answer sheets on my YouTube video: *A Gift for CA Final Students | Summary Notes of AIR 5 | Imp Section/Rule Name & No. and Case Laws.*

After Exams

I was so used to my 12-hour routine that the morning after my CA Final was over, I felt lost without anything to do. I was sad that there is no paper to give now LOL! So I took a week off and then returned to Mumbai to finish my articleship.

Now that we all have more free time, it's important to use it wisely and productively. To that end, I enrolled in some online courses. You can also use this time to consider what you want to do in the future. Keep yourself informed about current events. I suggest checking out channels like Dhruv Rathee, Think School, and StudyIQ, as well as podcasts from Bloomberg Quint. If you have a specific field in mind for your future, make sure you stay up-to-date in that area. Read current affairs related to it and dig deeper into the subject.

I took part in two national student paper conferences: one in Nashik and another in Thane. On 22nd December (a Sunday), I presented my paper on Transfer Pricing and GST at the CA student conference in Nashik. After working a Saturday on the 21st, I left Mumbai at 11 pm and prepared my PPT (16 slides) during the drive to Nashik. I arrived home at 3 am, rehearsed my paper thrice in an hour, and went to sleep at 4. I reached the destination by 10 am sharp the next morning and won the best paper presenter award. I left Nashik by 1 pm and arrived in Mumbai by 7 pm, as I had to go to work the next day.

I then hosted a CA student national conference on the 7th and 8th of January 2020. As the lead anchor, I had a lot of work to do. From editing the script to handling a crowd of 3200 students, it was challenging. We had to work on this after our office hours.

My point in sharing these stories is to demonstrate that if you have a goal in mind, you will find the best way to reach it. In the process, you will learn to prioritize your time.

The result day for CA Final was 16th January 2020. This time my dad found out both the day and the time of announcement haha! The result was to be announced at 4 in the evening.

I logged in and no prizes for guessing, the site crashed. Again. When I finally checked my result, it was 566/800.

The Institute of Chartered Accountants of India

Examination Results, November 2019

Logout

Final New Examination Results, November 2019

PASS WITH DISTINCTION

Roll Number	
Name	KUSHAL SANTOSH LODHA
Group I	
Financial Reporting	076
Strategic Financial Management	088
Advanced Auditing and Professional Ethics	059
Corporate and Economic Laws	055
Total	278
Result	PASS
Group II	
Strategic Cost Management and Performance Evaluation	064
Elective Paper [6A Risk Management]	073
Direct Tax Laws and International Taxation	065
Indirect Tax Laws	086
Total	288
Result	PASS
Grand Total	566

My CA Finals scorecard

I had failed to reach my target of 600. Nonetheless, my parents were really happy. My dad had tears in his eyes and my sister had already bought an Apple Watch Series 5 for me and asked her driver to drop it at my house as she was not in town. I got a call from the Vice Chairman of the Board of Studies congratulating me.

The proudest aspect of my performance was my AIR 5. I had really wanted to maintain the rank I had in IPCC and I had successfully done it. The feeling was so magical and wholesome that it cannot be expressed; it can only be felt.

Congratulatory calls started coming in from everywhere. Those relatives who had told me to enjoy my sister's wedding were the first ones to congratulate me. That is when I realized that everyone will take credit for your success but will distance themselves if you fail. Once again I was all over the hoardings in Nashik and also on news channels.

Getting a rank in CA Final comes with many advantages. You can be shortlisted by prestigious companies such as BCG, Bain, and McKinsey. You are likely to get jobs with good packages, but most importantly, you get to join the Management Development Program where all the rankers are invited. It's a 25-day program and is like a mini MBA.

In this program, we are prepared for upcoming interviews, group discussions, and how to build our resumes. We are given various case studies and asked to share our thoughts on them. This program is taught by retired IIM A professors who want to give back to society. There were 128 students during our time and we built strong connections in those 25 days.

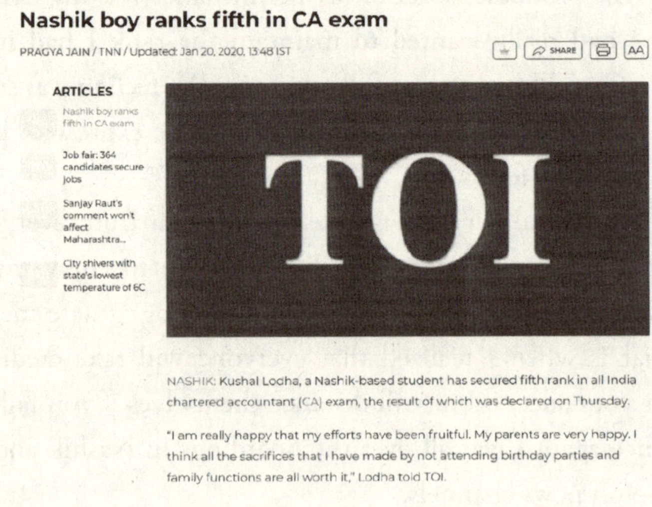

Nashik boy ranks fifth in CA exam

PRAGYA JAIN / TNN / Updated: Jan 20, 2020, 13:48 IST

SHARE AA

ARTICLES

Nashik boy ranks fifth in CA exam

Job fair: 364 candidates secure jobs

Sanjay Raut's comment won't affect Maharashtra...

City shivers with state's lowest temperature of 6C

NASHIK: Kushal Lodha, a Nashik-based student has secured fifth rank in all India chartered accountant (CA) exam, the result of which was declared on Thursday.

"I am really happy that my efforts have been fruitful. My parents are very happy. I think all the sacrifices that I have made by not attending birthday parties and family functions are all worth it," Lodha told TOI.

Featured in TOI after IPCC results

Contrary to popular belief, all the toppers were not boring bookworms. We were all very mischievous. I still remember that on my birthday, I was staying in the hostel and they made me dance to the song "Baby Doll".

Even if you're not a rank holder, you should still celebrate! You won't have the same advantages, but that doesn't mean you can't achieve your dreams. You can still get hired by companies like BCG and Bain, it just might take a bit longer. Reach out to their HRs on LinkedIn, and make a great pitch to consider you for the job.

But what if you fail? Remember that you're still just one step away from becoming a CA. The 1,440* hours you've put in won't be for nothing. Failing at CA Finals isn't the end of the world. Analyze your mistakes, practice more, and take the paper again. The victory you'll feel after overcoming failure will make all your hard work worth it. And keep practicing more!

Practice makes you better, if not perfect!

* Assuming you study for 12 hours a day for 4 consecutive months, this means 12 hours x 30 days x 4 months = 1,440 hours approximately. You have studied for 1,440 long hours.

9. Campus Placements - The Race for the Best Jobs

On the morning of February 25, 2020, just one day after my 21st birthday, the competition for the best jobs officially commenced. Enrolling in the CA management program and achieving a rank in the CA Final offers the benefit of participating in a special campus placement.

It was a nervy day. By 7 am, we were all aboard the bus which was supposed to take us to the venue of the placements, a 5-star hotel. About 15-20 companies such as Flipkart, Bajaj, ITC, and Deutsche Bank were present for the placements. The companies ended up conducting around 130 interviews on the day.

On this morning, I was surprised to learn that one

of my friends, Prateek Mandhane, had opted out of the placements. I called him up to enquire if everything was fine. His response was a moment of great learning for me. He wanted to set up his own practice and was going to do just that. He did not want to waste his own time or of any company that might have been interested in him. He was clear about the path he wanted to pursue. The takeaway here is that you should introspect and have a firm understanding of what you want to achieve and the core motivation behind chasing a company, a brand, or even an initiative of your own. Appear for interviews you really want a job in, and not just for the sake of practice.

On the day, I was shortlisted by 10 companies but I appeared for interviews with only 3 - Deutsche Bank, ITC, and Bajaj Auto Limited.

I have a few important pieces of advice about the placements here. Never put in a very high expected salary while filling out the campus placement forms. The ideal range of CTC expectation should be around Rs. 7 to Rs. 14 lakhs depending upon the company. I made the mistake of writing Rs. 20 lakhs as my expected CTC and thus got rejected by various companies. Also, if you mention that you are willing to relocate anywhere, your chances of making the shortlist are higher. If you are applying to a PSU, ensure that you fill in your graduation details otherwise they won't shortlist you. Select all the industries irrespective of where you want to work.

My friends and I were sitting in the lobby while each of us went through the different stages of placements. The calming lemongrass aroma of the lobby didn't help any of us with our nerves. Deutsche Bank had a 3-step interview process, which started with a group discussion. We were grouped together in batches of 10 for the discussions. My group's topic was the impact of GST on the Indian economy.

The following tips can help when participating in a group discussion:

- Don't turn a group discussion into a debate. Discussion and debate are two completely different things.
- Make sure that you speak your mind; interject others politely if you have to.
- The moderators want to evaluate your leadership abilities. Fit into the group but also show that you can be the leader.
- Your interjection and communication skills are evaluated. Articulate your thoughts in a precise manner. Try to lead the discussion and make others accept your point of view.

The next round was a personal interview with a panel.

Keep the following points in mind while appearing for a personal interview:

- DO NOT PANIC! Everyone is nervous and it's okay to be nervous. But if you panic, you signify that you can't handle the pressure that comes with the job.
- In the beginning of the interview, take the first 60-90 seconds to introduce yourself. That introduction should be like an elevator pitch - precise and to the point. In that, try to include some of your key achievements. These 90 seconds are your chance to set a good first impression.
- Maintain eye contact with the interviewers. If the question was asked to you by one interviewer, make sure while answering the question you make eye contact with every interviewer in the room.
- BE HONEST! If you don't know the answer to any question, don't blabber and bullshit your way through. Instead, just say that you don't know and will read up on it. Interviewers always prefer honesty.
- Listen closely to the introductions of your interviewers and always ask a question at the end. This shows that you are actually interested in the company and are serious about working there. It's good to have a list of pre-prepared questions to ask. Some of the questions I used to ask were:

  - How are the growth prospects in your company?
  - What are the skills you expect in a successful can-

didate?

- What does a typical work week look like in your company?

~

During my personal interview, I was asked a lot of technical questions and problems on mental maths. I answered to the best of my ability and told them honestly about the ones I was clueless. I cleared the second round of interviews too. The last round was based on current affairs. This is where it gets really tricky. I was asked questions like the difference between wholesale price and consumer price index, and about the corporate bank crisis in PMC Bank at that time. While I knew what was happening, I wasn't aware of the details. I didn't know the answer to important questions such as who the defaulter was and why the crisis happened.

Sadly, I couldn't clear the last round. Based on this experience, I highly recommend staying updated with the industry you are applying for. You should be aware of the major changes in the industry and why they are happening.

I was disheartened, to say the least. Working at Deutsche Bank was my dream and it was shattered into pieces. The rejection hit me hard. The fact that I didn't even get shortlisted by companies like HUL and Bain, as I hadn't done my articleship from BIG 4 and did a B.Com in correspondence, broke something in me. I started doubting myself. When I asked for feedback, all the Deutsche Bank executive said to me was, "All the best for your future endeavors." I had achieved a ranked at every level yet I got rejected. Did it mean that all I had was theoretical knowledge and no practical nous? Did I lack something necessary? Crippled with my self-doubts, I turned to my father for advice.

My father told me not to let rejection define my life. If I was turned down by one company, it wasn't the right fit for me; life had something else in store. Later, I learned that each company has its own criteria to fulfill. Failing to meet one company's standards doesn't mean you'll fail every opportunity.

A friend of mine was accepted at BCG but not at Bain, while another was accepted at Bain but not at BCG. Each company expects something different from candidates, and luck plays a role too. Not every day can be your day, and not every interview can be the one you crack.

Are you curious about the criteria for MNCs? While each company has its own standards, here are some of the basics I'm aware of:

- Companies usually prefer articleship from the Big 4,

though it's not mandatory if you have a strong CV from a mid-size firm.

- Extracurricular activities are essential. It's not enough to be an academic star; employers want an all-rounder. You should be strong in your studies, but also have experience in activities like presenting a paper, moderating events, or volunteering.
- A college degree is usually preferred over a correspondence degree. The idea is that if you attend college, you'll have more opportunities to hone your leadership skills through college activities. I regret not attending college for my B.Com; it's why I wasn't shortlisted by Bain and HUL.

~

I moved on from this initial disappointment and began preparing for my interview with ITC. It was the most difficult interview I had ever experienced. 45 minutes in, I was trembling with nervousness. Let me recount some details from the process.

Their group discussion was quite unique; instead of the usual political or current topic, we were given a scenario and had to decide who the murderer was from seven suspects. We had only 5 minutes to read the case, then had to articulate our thoughts and speak for 15-20 minutes. There was no right or wrong answer; they were testing how quickly we could think on our feet.

The GD was followed by a personal interview where I was asked the toughest technical questions covering topics like:

- Impact of IND AS 110 on listed entities
- Difference between Ind AS 115 and the previous Accounting Standard
- Why ICFR was bought in the Companies Act
- GST (I presented a paper on GST according to my resume. I was given a situation of their own company's case going on in high court and asked if I was the judge, what would have been my judgment?)
- Transfer pricing; I had to detail out a case study on this

They were testing my confidence and patience: how? By laying a trap. They asked me questions and challenged my answers, trying to see how long I could remain steadfast. I managed to stay strong for 45 minutes, but then my confidence wavered. As I left the interview room, my heart sank; I was sure I was going to receive another rejection.

5 minutes later, I received a call from the HR. At that moment, my heart was literally in my mouth. I was expecting a "we regret to inform you" but instead got "Congratulations! We are pleased to…" and I got a job

at ITC for an internal audit role. I was offered a CTC of Rs. 22 lakhs per annum. It was among the companies offering the highest packages. But unfortunately, the role was based out of Kolkata and I didn't wish to travel that far. Also, the role was for internal audit and I did not want to work in that domain. Nevertheless, I decided to keep this job on hold and continued with other interviews.

I applied for a vacancy in the Aditya Birla Group. ABG wasn't part of the campus placement process. I got to know about it through a WhatsApp group which had other CA rank holders and applied to both ABG and BCG from the information shared there.

Another approach is to send cold emails to HRs of these organizations. The best way to find an email id is to visit their LinkedIn handle first; for instance, type "BCG HR LinkedIn" on Google and you will get their LinkedIn handles. Then, type "BCG email domain address" to see what domain name is working at BCG. Mostly, you will get the results as "@bcg.com". Then verify whether the email id is valid or not. I use snov.io to check the validity of email addresses. Try some different permutations and combinations till you figure out the verified email id.

I had an interview with ABG on March 14, 2020. It was a 2-part process. The first round was an online assessment, which tested my knowledge in topics such as logical, inductive, and deductive reasoning. The second round was a personal interview, which lasted for about 55 minutes and was quite intense. It included a case study followed by a questioning round.

In the case study, I was given a 12-page case of a public company which wanted to go private. I had to conclude whether the decision was feasible. I had 30 minutes to go through the entire case and articulate my thoughts.

After the case study round, for the next 25 minutes, I was grilled on technical questions and current affairs. I was asked questions around:

- Difference between the cost of equity and the cost of reserves
- Difference between revenue and surplus
- What is CAPM?
- The Yes Bank crisis

The ABG selection did not go smoothly either. Approximately 130-140 people appeared for the online assessment of ABG. Out of these, only the top 30 were selected and called for the next round of interviews. I, unfortunately, did not make it to the top 30. I came 31st and was waitlisted. I did not have much hope but still texted the HR of ABG requesting them to consider me if there was a dropout. There were 8 people who had the same rank as mine. It so happened that there was a dropout amongst the top 30 and HR considered me for the opening amongst these 8. Well, I am not sure whether I should thank my stars or my well-drafted resume for this opportunity.

The hidden gem while applying for a job or sitting in an interview is your resume. Your resume should be as good as it can be. It should be a single-pager, in a simple format using short and crisp sentences, with all your achievements highlighted. Use as many numbers as possible to validate your claims. But most importantly use keywords, good keywords. It should also contain:

- Results of 10th, 12th, B.Com, and CA
- Your experience in a reversed chronological order
- Extra-curricular activities

I've shared my resume on the next page.

Having a well-drafted resume is essential, but being knowledgeable about its contents is just as important. Interviewers often ask questions based on what is listed on your resume. For example, I was asked questions about GST during my ITC interview, as I had mentioned mentioned about a paper I presented on this topic on my resume. My friend, who was a national-level cricketer, was asked questions about cricket, such as defining what a 'long on' position is on the field. Therefore, it is important to be aware of the information you include on your resume.

Kushal Lodha | Male | 22

PROFESSIONAL AND ACADEMIC CREDENTIALS

COURSE	YEAR	INSTITUTION	MARKS (%)	REMARKS
ACCA	Sept 2021	Association of Chartered Certified Accountants	311 / 400 (77.8%)	**All India Rank – 4**
CA Final	Nov 2019	The Institute of Chartered Accountants of India	566 / 800 (70.8%)	**All India Rank – 5**
CFA Level II	June 2019	CFA Institute	Pass	Above 90 percentile
CFA Level I	June 2018	CFA Institute	Pass	Above 90 percentile
B.Com	2016 – 2019	Savitribai Phule Pune University	821 / 1200 (68.4%)	-
Actuarial Science	2016 – present	Institute of Actuaries of India	Pass	Cleared 5 Levels
CA Intermediate	Nov 2016	The Institute of Chartered Accountants of India	541 / 700 (77.3%)	**All India Rank – 5**
CA Foundation	Dec 2015	The Institute of Chartered Accountants of India	186 / 200 (93.0%)	**All India Rank – 6**
A Levels - Class XII	Nov 2015	Fravashi International Academy, Nashik	440 / 500 (88.0%)	3rd in Class
IGCSE – Class X	Nov 2013	Fravashi International Academy, Nashik	834 / 900 (92.7%)	2nd in Class

WORK EXPERIENCE

Aditya Birla Group – Finance Leadership Program (Jun'20 – Present)

Current Role – EA to Chief Economist, Aditya Birla Group (Jun'21 – Present)

- Assisted **Capital Requisite Evaluation Committee** to **approve capital expansion** of **$1 billion** for **Paints business** and **$100 million** for **Yarn business**
- Assisting in **Macroeconomic projections and analysis** for planning and budgeting of **Grasim Industries Limited,** having a **turnover** of **$10 billion**
- **Represented to Ministry of Commerce and Industry** for supporting businesses to **analytically rationalize and champion the policy advocacy** needs
- Updating businesses on **financial markets development** by conducting **monthly meetings and knowledge sessions**
- **Writing articles** and **recording monthly podcasts with the Chief Economist** on **current affairs** to be circulated to **5,500 employees** of the Group

ABFRL, Louis Philippe (Feb'21 – May'21)

- Analyzing **sales data**, at every **shop-in-shop till Contribution before Advertisement (CBA) level**, with multiple factors like **revenue generation, margins, discount, return,** etc.
- Analysis of **negative factors** leading to **erosion of CBA**

Corporate Finance (Oct'20 – Jan'21)

- Identified potential **FinTech** (having approximate **valuation** of **$500 million**) **partnership opportunities** for **NBFC business** of **Aditya Birla Capital**
- Prepared various **financial models of new-age businesses** of the Group to evaluate project feasibility
- Assisted in **sell-side diligence** of sale of **Grasim Fertilizers business** to **Indorama Corp. Pte Ltd.** for **$350 million**

Strategy & Business Development, Aditya Birla Capital (Jun'20 – Sep'20)

- Conducting **due diligence of Business Correspondents** to explore partnerships in order to expand the reach of **NBFC business of Aditya Birla Capital** into **Tier II & Tier III** cities
- Identifying and analyzing **M&A opportunities** for **NBFC and HFC** businesses of Aditya Birla Capital

Gokhale & Sathe, Chartered Accountants, Mumbai – Articled Assistant (Apr'17 – Mar'20)

Area of work	- Handled **Direct Taxation Assessment** and **Litigation** before the **Commissioner of Income Tax (Appeals)** and **attended hearings** in the **Income Tax Appellate Tribunal** - Engaged into **advisory** of the **Domestic Income Tax** as well as **International Tax** - Involved in **advisory and compliance** related to **Goods and Services Tax** - Integral team member of **Statutory Audit Assignment of a Co-operative Bank** (having an **asset base of $1.2 billion**)

AWARDS, ACHIEVEMENTS AND SKILLS

Significant Scholastic Awards & Recognitions	- **"Youth Icon of Nashik"** in 2019 organized by Radio Mirchi 98.3 FM for inspiring the young generation of the Nashik City - **National Topper** in **Accounting** in AS Level (Class XI) in **Nov 2015** - **National Topper** in **Additional Mathematics** in IGCSE (Class X) in **Nov 2013** - Awarded as **"Champion"** in **UCMAS Abacus** in Nashik – a contest on **Mental Mathematics**
Technical Skills	- Proficient in **Bloomberg, Tracxn, Private Circle, Statista, CMIE, MS-Excel, MS-Word** and **MS-PowerPoint** - Completed a course on **"Financial Modeling"** on **Udemy**

Other Extra-Curricular Activities	- Run a **podcast on YouTube** (**Channel Name – Kushal Lodha**) with a **current subscriber base** of **70k** and have interviewed eminent personalities like **Shri. Suresh Prabhu, Shri. TN Manoharan, Mr. R Gopalakrishnan,** and **Mr. Shailesh Haribhakti**
	- **Core Committee member** of **Seminar, Public Relations & Membership Development Committee** of **Bombay Chartered Accountants' Society**, a voluntary organization **established in 1949** having more than **10,000 members**
	- Assisted as an **Educator on Unacademy,** India's largest learning platform, in **May 2020**
	- **Lead Anchor** at the **National Conference for CA Students' 2020** where **3,200 students** had attended the conference
	- **Core Committee Member** of **'Aagaaz'** in **Jan 2020,** an annual fest for CA students in Mumbai where **1,000 students** had attended the **4-day event**
	- **Best Paper Presenter** in **CA Students' Conference**
	    o Thane (Dec 2019) – Allowance and Disallowance of Input Tax Credit
	    o Nashik (Dec 2019) – Transfer Pricing and Domestic Transfer Pricing
	    o Thane (Dec 2018) – Income Tax Supreme Court landmark judgments
	- **Best Presenter** in **Management and Communication Skills** organized by ICAI in Feb, 2019
	- Awarded as **"High Commendation"** and **"Special Mentions"** in **Model United Nations (Nashik MUN 2014 & 2015)**
	- Represented my school at **District Level Cricket and Chess Competition** in 2010
	- **Co-curricular Activities Captain** in **Grade VIII**

I was grateful to get a chance to appear for the interview at ABG. After I exited the interview room, I was really nervous because other people came out in only half an hour while mine ran for nearly an hour. This time I didn't make any assumptions about my rejection or selection. I was just blank on emotions and moved on to prepare for my upcoming interview at BCG.

After two days, the results of the ABG interviews were released. Of the 30 shortlisted candidates, only 5 were selected, and I was one of them. I was offered a CTC of Rs. 18.25 lakhs per annum. With two offers in hand, I was filled with confidence as I appeared for my BCG interview, a company I had long dreamed working for.

The interview process at BCG was unique. I had been used to hour-long interviews, but the process at BCG was a month-long! BCG has a "buddy" concept, which is designed to help applicants prepare for their interviews. This buddy is usually a Consultant who has been working at the company for 2-3 years and has solved many case studies. They are well-equipped to help us prepare for our case studies and the interview process.

For my interview, I solved a total of 190 case studies with my friends and the support of my assigned buddy. Interviewers aren't looking for a correct answer, as there isn't one necessarily. Instead, they assess your ability to organize and articulate your thoughts in a structured manner. For example, if the case study is something like "estimate the number of golf balls in the air in India right now" or "estimate the number of poha particles in a plate", you should ensure that you present your assumptions and ideas in a structured way. The interviewer is more interested in the structure of your thoughts than the answer itself.

I used to take feedback and recommendations from my buddy and friends, and act on them. Rectifying mistakes is essential. To prepare for BCG interview case studies, the best book is "Case Interviews Cracked". I solved the whole book. Before reading the solution, I structured my thoughts on paper and then compared them to the provided solution. I really worked hard for this interview.

The case studies that I was asked about were the following:

a) Estimate the perfume market size in India.

I went about solving it in the following manner.

- Divide the entire population between rural and urban. Then into males and females.
- Further divide into the age-wise category like 18-24, 24-60, and so on.
- Assume how many people from these brackets would use perfume.
- Multiply that number by the cost of perfume.
- Replacement of perfume every year x 3 (assuming that people use 3 bottles of perfume every year) leading to an increase in the market size.

b) The profit of a stationery shop in school was

declining. Give recommendations.

c) Estimate the Whiskey market of India.

(Since I had no idea about the prices for alcohol, I asked the interviewer at the start only about the prices and then went about solving the case.)

d) Baskin Robins wanted to set up operations across India. Advise on how they can go ahead.

This was the case study in which I forgot to ask the basic question of the locations BR wanted to be in, and also didn't take into account the aspects of dine-in and take-out. This was where I failed the interview. BCG was kind enough to give me feedback. They stated they wouldn't be comfortable placing me in front of their clients and suggested I work on my communication skills.

I was heartbroken. BCG was my dream job and I failed to crack its interview because I overlooked the basics. I couldn't even apply to BCG for the next two years because of their cooling-off policy. Nevertheless, I learned another important lesson from this experience - "observation". During that one month, I and all my friends became so observant that we would make up case studies and discuss business problems like management consultants. I realized that staying observant at all times helps you look at things from a broader perspective, analyze improvement opportunities, and most importantly, learn something incremental in return.

Nowadays, this small habit of observation has been lost. When travelling alone in a cab, people just squander their time away on their mobile phones. The same can be said for when waiting outside a doctor's clinic or a café for a friend who is running late.

Developing the habit of observation can quickly cultivate the skill of curiosity. The more observant you are, the more likely you are to become inquisitive and creative since you have seen more than others. For instance, how those attractive clothes are displayed on the mannequin to catch a customer's attention so that they can enter the store, or how chocolate wrappers are packed to make it more convenient for the consumer to open and eat are some simple examples of tactics used by companies to improve their sales! The better the solution, the more obscure its implementation, so much so that we often fail to notice such minute details.

"Strategy requires thoughts, tactics require observation!" And only a blend of good strategy with amazing tactics will help an organization prosper.

When I was rejected by BCG, I was heartbroken but now in retrospect, I think it was a boon in disguise. If I would have gone to BCG, I wouldn't have had the time for anything else. BCG has a crazy number of working hours. If I would have spent 18 hours on my office work, I would have never reached where I am today on Youtube, Instagram, and LinkedIn. It was for the best that I joined the Aditya Birla Group.

On the next page, I have listed the packages some top companies give to its freshers, as of 2022.

Getting placed is a landmark moment in every student's life. If you've landed your dream job, congratulations! It's time to celebrate! If you haven't landed your dream job, but still got into a company, you should still celebrate. There's a lot of hype initially about brands and packages, but in the long run, it's your experience and skills that matter. There are pros and cons to each type of job when you begin. In the early years of your career, focus on learning and building skills, and everything else will follow.

Work hard to get what you like otherwise you'll be forced to like what you get!

Company	Approximate Package offered (per annum)
Marico	Rs. 30 Lakhs
HUL	Rs. 27 Lakhs
ITC	Rs. 22 Lakhs
Desutsche Bank	Rs. 22 Lakhs
Aditya Birla Group	Rs. 18.25 Lakhs
JP Morgan	Rs. 20 Lakhs (including bonus)
Bank of America	Rs. 35 Lakhs
Mondelez	Rs. 20 Lakhs
BCG	Rs. 18 Lakhs
Bain	Rs. 16 Lakhs
ONGC	Rs. 20 Lakhs
Big 4s	Rs. 6 – 10 Lakhs

Approximate fresher CTCs of top companies

10. Setting the Foundation - First Job at ABG

Student life was over. It was time to face the real world. The real 'real world'. Articleship was just a taste of it. This was the complete meal. No more classes and exams, it was time to translate all those years of academic rigour to actual, practical value.

My first job was with the coveted, prestigious Aditya Birla Group. Just being associated with this name was a matter of pride. After receiving a confirmation call from ABG on 16th March 2020, I was to join the office on 8th June. I was selected for their Management Trainee program where we work in three stints of four months each.

As I was looking forward to this new chapter in my

life, Covid knocked on our doors and wreaked havoc. My dreams of working in the cushy office of ABG were quashed, and I started out in front of my computer screen sitting my room.

In May and June 2020, I had an unexpected feeling of freedom. Looking for something productive to do, I was fortunate to be contacted by Unacademy. They asked me to give lectures on SFM, and since I had the time and was interested in trying something new, I accepted. I taught SFM to 15-20 CA Final students for one hour a day, unaware of the market rate for teaching. I agreed to the nominal charge of Rs. 1,000/- per hour. My short stint at Unacademy was a rewarding experience; I received positive feedback and was even ranked the number 2 CA teacher. In June, I had to leave Unacademy to join my actual job.

~

In Christianity, baptism is a ritual in which water is sprinkled on the forehead of a baby, symbolizing their regeneration and admission into the Christian church. Similarly, when a student enters the corporate world, they are "baptized by fire" - a metaphor for the challenges and difficulties they will face. Usually, their boss acts as the "priest" of this baptism.

I joined the Aditya Birla Group on June 8, 2020 online. My first four months were a period of intense learning. It was similar to my first introduction to corporate life in articleship - I got assigned to a very strict manager. On my first day, he asked if I understood SEBI, LODR, and ICDR regulations. I replied that I did understand them, but I would need to brush up on my skills. He scolded me pretty badly, saying that I should have come prepared. This is the real world and school was over.

The scolding and reprimands were routine features of my professional life early on. Every alternate day, I'd give some reason for my manager to dress me down. Once, I had just taken a break and was leaving for my lunch when he called. He told me to work on something that had to be sent immediately to the CEO. I responded by asking, "Okay, can I please do it in half an hour after I finish my lunch?" He got royally pissed with my answer and I could sense him fuming. "Are you out of your mind?? Did you not hear a word that I just said?? This is something that has to be sent to the CEO! You will start working on it RIGHT NOW!" He almost emerged out of the phone and gave me a tight slap. I was completely shaken. I sprinted back to my room and worked for two hours straight on a grumbling stomach.

I would dread any emails from my manager in my

inbox and feared his calls even more. Any form of communication meant trouble for me. I wondered if I was the only one getting this treatment or if others were also given this baptism by fire. I spoke to my friend Aakash Raka who was working in the wealth management sector, and I was relieved to know that he too was sailing in a similar boat. His manager had apparently told him once, "I have 99 problems in my life, and solving yours isn't one of them." Quite savage, I must say.

In my third month of working under the Assistant Vice President, I had made up my mind to quit. I couldn't take it any longer. My dad listened to me patiently as I shared my struggles with him. When I was done, he advised me to develop thicker skin. He said I wouldn't survive in this world if I chose to quit every time things got tough.

Those four months were a blessing in disguise. Look at it this way: for steel to become strong, it must endure high temperatures. And for us, there was no better way to learn than this baptism by fire. When you are pushed out of your comfort zone, you develop an entrepreneurial mindset.

I couldn't turn to my manager for help with doubts or confusion; instead, I had to do my own research. I read hundreds of websites, read research papers, watched YouTube videos, and talked to my friends to clear up any questions I had. Most of the time, in the process of clearing my doubts, I ended up learning even more about the subject.

During my first four-month tenure at ABG, I worked on mergers and acquisitions, peer benchmarking, and finding business correspondents for NBFCs. I was assigned three tasks.

My first task was to identify Non-Banking Financial Companies (NBFCs) and Housing Finance Companies (HFCs) that ABG, as a builder capital entity, could acquire or merge with. My second task was to analyze business correspondents with whom we could partner or integrate. For those unfamiliar, correspondents are people who help improve the retail presence of a bank or an NBFC. Lastly, I was tasked with peer benchmarking. I had to identify key ratios such as net interest margin, cost-income ratio, NPA ratio, and other parameters that are relevant to NBFCs.

After those four months, I was transferred to the Corporate Finance department from November 2020 to February 2021. I had survived the worst and was hopeful for a smoother journey ahead. My new manager treated me well and I got along with him. My work profile included M&A transactions for group companies, investment transactions, and involvement in deals. I also prepared daily capital market update reports. I updated the entire report sheet from the Bloomberg terminal and circulated it to all ABG employees. This work came with a lot of responsibility, as any mistake would be detected by everyone. Therefore, I had to be extremely thorough. Additionally, I updated ABG's investor presentation.

~

As much as this stint was the best of all professionally, it was personally the toughest. During those four months, my entire family contracted COVID-19, except for me. All of them were hospitalized. I had to move to my sister's house. During this difficult period, I learned two very important lessons.

The first was the importance of organizational support. My colleagues were not just coworkers, but also friends. They went above and beyond to cover for me, working overtime and even doing my job. They worked hard, but without recognition, claiming that I had done the work. I'm forever grateful for their help and support during this tough time.

The second lesson was the importance of doing multitasking well. I owe this to my sister. She managed to look after our parents, run her start-up, and make homemade food for everyone, all on her own. She had her priorities set and divided her attention between all of her tasks perfectly.

~

My last four-month stint was with Louis Philippe. I was tasked with investigating the loss-making store and identifying the cause. This required a lot of research. I had to put myself in the customer's shoes and consider their opinion of the brand. Unfortunately, due to the COVID-19 pandemic, I was unable to do as much groundwork as I would have liked. However, I did visit the Louis Philippe stores in Nashik and spoke to as many customers as I could.

Ironically, although this stint required me to do a lot of groundwork, it was still the most relaxed period yet. My manager had resigned, so I had no one to report to. I wasn't assigned any tasks, so I didn't do any work for those four months. Instead, I took the opportunity to focus on other things I wanted to do but couldn't due to my busy work schedule. I started learning guitar, something I had longed to do for a long time. I also paid attention to my physical health and joined a gym. Most importantly, I dedicated my attention to my content creation, as I had much more free time. I built my side hustle and worked on it, and this was when my social presence began to take off. I became more consistent with my content creation.

~

In the next six months, I was hired as the Executive Assistant to ABG's Chief Economist, Dr. Ajit Ranade. Before offering me the job, he conducted a one-hour interview. This was unlike any I had experienced during my campus placement or articleship. He asked me about my passions, extracurricular activities, and more. These questions were designed to assess my character. It was here that I learned that the behavioral aspect of a person is more important than technical knowledge. After an hour, he was impressed and offered me the job.

I was given more responsibilities when I was promoted to a higher job. I prepared economic research notes for all ABG employees and volunteered to create podcasts with Dr. Ajit Ranade for everyone to watch. I also took on projects such as forecasting necessary inputs and outputs for the group companies, analyzing cotton prices, and forecasting prices for fiber for the next three years.

In addition, my tasks included preparing minutes for board meetings, making briefing notes, conducting research, and helping Dr. Ranade with articles for publications like Livemint, Economic Times, and Times of

India. This was a complete research-based position.

Dr. Ajit Ranade epitomized the phrase "no matter how high you reach, keep your feet on the ground," which was evident in his down-to-earth attitude. A few lessons I learned while working with him closely are:

- Maintain composure, even in the most stressful situations; otherwise, you will make mistakes.
- Make reading a fixed, non-negotiable activity in your daily routine. Mental exercise is just as important as physical exercise.
- Love what you do and do what you love; otherwise, you will never enjoy life.
- This world runs on trust; it can be either 0% or 100% - nothing in between. For example, if a kid buys a pen for ₹20 from a stationery shop, the shopkeeper could argue that he never received cash, but there was trust between the kid and the shopkeeper. Because of this, the kid would go back to the same shop to buy again.
- Always question until you are satisfied with the answer; otherwise, you will not survive.
- Always keep the kid in your heart alive. No matter how successful you become, never let go of that inner child.

I feel extremely lucky to have closely worked with him. In fact, when I wished him "Happy Guru Purnima", he replied, "Happy Guru Purnima to you too". This exemplified his humility and the attitude to be a lifelong learner.

With Dr. Ajit Ranade

Although my CA degree taught me so much academically, only textbook knowledge would have made zero impact on this role. It was far beyond the scope of a traditional CA. I had to teach myself everything and conduct my own research. It was a tough challenge, but I really enjoyed it. The CA experience of learning large volumes of content by myself helped me perform this role well.

It's a myth that once you enter the corporate world, you no longer need to study. As a CA, you must always stay up-to-date and be knowledgeable in your field. I had to do a lot of research for the tasks I was assigned. In my last job, I had to read a lot, including reports of up to 400 pages long. Developing the habit of reading is essential, as it will benefit you throughout your career.

~

After finishing my stint as the EA to the Chief Economist of ABG, I applied to Aditya Birla Ventures, the newly formed VC fund of the Aditya Birla Group.

Venture capitalism was a new field for me and beyond my comfort zone. But we already know that growth is inversely proportional to the size of one's comfort zone. So, I went ahead. Aditya Birla Ventures was the new offshoot of ABG and the entire team was hired afresh, consisting of young professionals. We were all learning and growing together, and our bond quickly developed into a strong friendship. Working with people you consider family makes work feel less like a job and more like a passion.

The exposure at ABV was incredible. I had the opportunity to meet hundreds of startup founders. I gained invaluable insights into entrepreneurship. We'd receive thousands of pitches from founders, from which we had to select a few for callbacks and interviews, ultimately investing in one. By selecting projects for funding, I learned a great deal about doing a pitch that was comprehensive and had no loose ends. I developed a questioning mindset, as I had to constantly probe the founders on why we should invest in their projects. I had to prepare myself similarly when pitching the startup to our investors.

After working at ABG for two years, I learned several key facts. Irrespective of your manager's style, it's important to ensure clear communication between you and your manager. If you don't know what is expected of you, you won't be able to do your best. To meet your manager's expectations, you need to understand them well. Miscommunication between you and your manager can lead to a bad experience for both of you.

I also learned to always bring something extra to the table. Don't be afraid to speak your mind in meetings.

It's important to express your opinion, even if it seems silly, as it could have a positive impact on the company or someone else. Most organizations are successful because they value their employees' opinions and are open to suggestions. This increases the organization's involvement with employees while motivating them to contribute and work more efficiently.

In my opinion, employee satisfaction is more important than customer satisfaction. If employees are satisfied, customers will be satisfied in the end.

There is an interesting incident about how valuing employee opinions can sometimes make a massive impact. A relatively junior employee at Colgate Palmolive once suggested making the holes of their toothpaste bigger. This would result in a larger quantity of toothpaste coming out with each use, leading to higher sales and shorter repeat sales periods. The management heard him and implemented this suggestion. The brand saw a return to revenue and profitability growth, which had been a struggle prior. The employee, who was in an operations role, was in the best position to advise on this turnaround due to his understanding of the product's intricacies.

To have your opinion respected, it's equally important to articulate it clearly. I used to ramble on for 10-15 minutes during calls, but my manager advised me to be more direct. In the corporate world, it's essential to be precise and to the point. People are busy and impatient and appreciate only crisp communication.

I believe that regardless of whether you want to run your own practice or live the corporate life, you should definitely work in a job for one or two years. I worked at ABG for two years and the experience allowed me to understand the complexities of the corporate world. It gave me an insight into so many small and large aspects that result in the successful execution of business. I also made many meaningful connections and expanded my network. I made wonderful memories, grew personally and developed through difficult times.

However, despite the great experience and growth, I also realized working in a stable job wasn't my calling. It was time for me to move on. To hopefully bigger things.

Finally, I quit my job on 30th June 2022 and headed towards a new journey in my life!

At ABG

11. Busting the CA Myths

In my series 'Konversation with Kushal', Dr. Niranjan Hiranadani shared an amazing piece of advice for all the CA aspirants. He said, "Start loving what you learn. Students often look at the classes and exams as an enemy to beat, but the moment you immerse in them completely, it grows on you. And the subject becomes easier and easier to learn once you are actually passionate about the idea. So instead of thinking 'Oh my God, this is the mountain that I have to climb', you need to say, 'WOW! This is another mountain to climb!' That's the right attitude!"

CA is undoubtedly a tough mountain to climb, but it has been engulfed by so many myths that the climb seems tougher than it actually is. Most of these myths are actually *mithya*.

I have tried to bust these myths throughout the book but there are still many others which need to be addressed. Let's get to them.

CAs are Boring

The world outside has this perception that CAs are boring nerds with zero social skills and no sense of humour. You probably know that's not true, and luckily, there are so many CAs proving this wrong. Aman Gupta, co-founder and CMO of Boat, and easily the most chilled-out shark in the Shark Tank, is a prime example.

Yes, we have to study a lot of theory but we also have practical knowledge. Three years of articleship makes us street-smart too. In fact, no other professional degree accords such a long time of learning in the industry.

And we are definitely not all obedient pets who haven't broken any rules in life. I had my fair share of adventure during my hostel and had so many friends far more prone to trouble. We knew how to have fun.

We would go on late-night strolls along Juhu beach, and sometimes party late into the night. We prepared fake letters of absence and bribed the security guards to let us enter past curfew. This was true even for the apparently nerdy rank holders. Calling them boring would be a crime.

Everyone has their own definition of enjoyment. Just because something doesn't fit your definition doesn't mean it's boring. For example, a lot of friends went to a Post Malone concert in Mumbai, but I don't enjoy attending such events. It's not that I don't like music, I just don't find it exciting. I've never been to a cricket match either, even though I love playing the game. I just don't find it stimulating. The last time I went clubbing was around six months ago, and my friends have stopped inviting me since then. I also didn't follow the FIFA World Cup.

Many of you may have already judged me and labeled me as a "boring" person. But, I'm in love with my life as it is. I have no complaints or demands. I enjoy going to the gym and working out in the morning. I read 50 pages of a book each day, which serves as a mental exercise. Every night at 9:30 pm, I play table tennis for 30 minutes to refresh my mind. I cherish my mental peace and spend 15 minutes meditating every morning. My point is, we should let everyone live their life the way they want, rather than judging based on what is deemed "cool" in society. What is cool for you may not be cool for me. We need to accept this and let each of us have our own ways of having fun.

If you are living by someone else's definition of

being cool, then you are actually a fool!

CA course is not worth it and will not have much demand in the future!

I often get asked by students whether they should pursue CA or go for other similar courses like CFA, FRM, CFP, CMT, etc. The primary reason this is asked is that completing CA takes 5 years of toil while the other courses can be finished in a much shorter period.

While other courses are undoubtedly shorter in duration, they also don't usually get you as high-paying a job as the CA course does. In my opinion, these courses should be done in supplement to CA and not in isolation.

If I take my own example, I spent a total of Rs. 3.5 Lakhs on my entire CA journey over 5 years, after which I got my first job of Rs. 18.25 Lakhs per annum! You're smart enough to compute the ROI and THAT answers whether doing a CA is worth it or not.

Also, as more and more people start paying taxes in India, and as the tax to GDP ratio of our country which is at a record high of 11.7% (as of April 2022) continues rising, the demand for CAs will only increase in the future.

CAs will not only be needed in traditional fields of taxation and auditing but also in areas like SAP implementation, Forensic Auditing, Artificial Intelligence, etc.

I'm very confident that the demand of CAs and the earning potential for them will continue to grow as our nation progresses to newer heights. In conclusion, this course is surely worth the toil of 5 years!

If you've done your articleship in taxation, you'll only be considered for taxation jobs.

I repeat it again. CA makes you the jack of all trades and the master of one. If you have done your articleship in a specific department, it doesn't mean you have to work in that department for life, unless that's what you want. I did my articleship in departments like Auditing, GST, and Direct Tax but ended up doing completely different things at my job in Aditya Birla Group. I had never worked in the economic or venture capital divisions before.

Only two things matter - your skills and your interest in a particular field. If you have both, nothing can stop you from succeeding in your preferred field, regardless of where you did your articleship.

MBA is preferred over CA

For a long time, there has been a rivalry of sorts between MBA and CA. It is true that historically MBAs have been preferred over CAs. Some companies used to keep

MBA graduates in client-facing roles while CAs were restricted to backend jobs.

In 2016 at the CA convocation ceremony in which my friend also convocated, Mr. Sridhar Vembu, the founder of Zoho, was the keynote speaker. During his speech, he said that CAs are not problem solvers but finders. And my friend stood up and responded, "If you can't find the problem, you won't be able to solve it."

However, the gap between finding and solving problems is shrinking day by day. CAs are now being expected to find the problems and then articulate them well. They are rigorously trained for this now. Moreover, with the management trainee programs, CAs are at par with MBAs. A CA rank holder's package at ABG is the same as that of an IIM graduate.

Furthermore, in the near future, ICAI's curriculum will become more practical-oriented, eliminating the preference of MBAs for front desk jobs.

CAs can only be CFOs

It's all about how big your cup of ambition is. CAs aren't just limited to the role of CFOs. In fact, many of the Chairmen and CEOs of companies are CAs. Look at Mr. Deepak Parekh, Mr. Kumar Mangalam Birla and Mr. T.N. Manoharan. All of them are CAs.

To become a CEO, you must go beyond the typical

CFO role and set high standards for yourself. It takes more than just a title to be a successful CEO; you must possess unique skills and deep knowledge of the industry. Furthermore, strong communication skills are essential for leading a company.

How can you bring something unique to the table? To stand out from the crowd, you must do what others don't want to do. When assigned a task, such as creating a presentation on a certain topic, you must give it your all.

What does that mean? Of course, you need to put in the hours, but you should also do some smart work. Research the topic, listen to podcasts, watch YouTube videos, and read up on news related to it. Most importantly, ask your colleagues and friends for their views. By incorporating different perspectives into your presentation, you can gain a better understanding of the topic.

The combination of hard work and smart work is what will make you stand out and justify any role you undertake with flying colours - whether CFO or CEO.

It's very difficult to clear the CA exam

It's a myth that it is difficult to clear the CA exam. It is not so hard to do so; I have done it, and so have many others. It all depends on how well you manage your workload, studies, and mindset.

To help you prepare, here are some pointers:

- Give yourself 3-4 months of dedicated preparation.
- Study qualitatively, not quantitatively.
- Talk to only a few people and focus on solving each other's doubts, rather than gossiping or discussing movies.
- The fewer people you talk to, the more peaceful your life will become. This will save you time and energy.
- Sacrifice some of the things that eat into your productivity, otherwise what you want will become the sacrifice.
- ICAI material is the Bible, stick to it.
- Plan well and execute it consistently, daily.

But, hey, this is my opinion and you don't necessarily need to adhere to it. Follow what works for you the best. All I can say is that with well-directed, focused and consistent effort, this exam can be easily cracked.

Most people will say:
"Discipline is boring,
Studying is boring,
CA Course is boring!"
Tell them, "Boring things make you successful!"

12. What Else Can You Do with CA?

If you have the desire to learn, there's always abundant knowledge available for you to consume and absorb. In this chapter, I have listed courses that you can take along with or after completing CA. But I have a strong word of advice - don't simply take these additional courses under peer pressure, FOMO, or ego. Degrees don't define you. The impact you make with (or without) them does. So if you are not deeply interested in the subject, don't waste your time on it.

For all these supplementary courses, I have added details on the eligibility, exam patterns and registration fees, the area of Interest the course corresponds to, its scope for a CA post-completion, and possible job roles that the course can help you pursue. I hope the content helps you identify the right courses you may wish to pursue from the plethora of options available today.

~

1. *CFA*

- Eligibility: Your selected exam window must be 23 months or fewer before your graduation month for your bachelor's degree or equivalent program. You must also complete your degree program prior to the date of sitting for your Level II exam. Basically, you can appear for Level I in your 2nd year, and register for Level II even while you are in your 3rd year but can appear for Level II only if you have completed your graduation.
- Area of interest: Finance
- Exam pattern: There are 3 Levels
  - Conducted in February, May, August and November for Level 1
  - Conducted in May, August and November for Level 2
  - Conducted in February and August for Level 3
- Fees: $3,000 - $4,000
- Scope for a CA: Since this is a global course, your

chances of getting jobs internationally become higher with CFA. Moreover, it gives you an edge in getting shortlisted for roles in Private Equity and Venture Capital firms.

- Possible roles you can consider post-completion:
  - Portfolio Manager
  - Risk Analyst/ Risk Manager
  - Research Analyst
  - Investment Banker
  - Private wealth Manager
- Ultimately, if you want to be a specialist in finance, go for CFA! Most people enroll for CFA only because of FOMO! They see other CAs doing it and follow along without inherent interest. Do not do this ever!

2. *LAW*

- Eligibility: Degree from a recognized university
- Area of interest: If you are fascinated by the legal topics in the CA course and want to pursue law as a major in your career, then this course is for you.
- Possible roles include specialized practice in one or more of the following:
  - Corporate law
  - Civil law
  - International law
  - Labor law

  - Family law
  - Patent law, etc.
- Possible job profiles:
  - Lawyers
  - Judges
  - Legal Advisors
  - Legal Executives
  - Solicitors
- Scope after CA+LLB: You can potentially attract more customers and provide them with a wider range of services. The demand for CAs with a degree in law is high in the market. A law degree will broaden your service scope to include even the legalities of the company. Companies will also prefer CA+LLB for the wider range of expertise.
- By the way, let me give you a surprise as well. I am also currently (early 2023) in my 2nd year of Law in GLC (Government's Law College) in Mumbai and haven't appeared for my exams because of other work. However, I hope I will finish it in the near future, haha!

3. *MBA*

- Eligibility: Degree from a recognized university
- Area of Interest: Business
- Possible domains to consider post-completion:

- Banking
- Consulting
- Finance
- Human resource
- Marketing and operations
- Digital Marketing

- Roles after MBA:
  - Management Consultant
  - Project Manager
  - Business Development Executive/ Manager
  - Product Manager
  - Marketing Manager
  - Analytics Manager
  - System Manager
  - Data Processing Manager
  - Business Analyst
- Fees: Rs. 20-25 Lakhs for 2 years if you are doing it from Tier 1 college in India. However, the fees would range from $100,000 to $150,000 if you go for an Ivy League University.
- Synergy of CA+MBA: It aids the transition across functions, and opens a wider range of job opportunities. MBA helps inculcate strategic thinking, analytical and communication skills.
- If you're considering an MBA, try to do it from a Tier 1 institute. That will add more value to your

career in the future.

4. *FRM*

- Eligibility: Anyone in the first year of your graduation or beyond can sit for level 1.
- Area of interest: Risk Management, Financial Modelling, and Valuations
- Exam pattern: Has "2" part exams followed by "2" years of Work Experience. Held twice a year – Around May and November.
- Fees: ~$1000 for Part 1, ~$600 for Part 2
- Possible roles post-completion:
    - Financial Risk/Manager
    - Enterprise Risk Management
    - Investment Banking
    - Trading
    - Wealth Management
    - Other roles involving Capital Markets

5. *CIMA*

- Eligibility:
    - Completed high school
    - Undergrad degree
    - MBA (beneficial for quicker enrollment)
    - Pursuing or pursued any professional degree
- Fields of employment: Accounting and auditing

- Fees: £2,500 – £3,000
- Possible roles post-completion:
  - Finance Manager
  - Management Consultant
  - Management Accountant
  - Finance Business Partner
  - Financial Accountant
  - Business Analyst
  - Accounts Assistant
  - Project Manager
  - Forensic Accountant
- Insight: CIMA is a fantastic course to pursue together with CA. Additionally, it is a curriculum that is widely accepted, which may increase the range of roles you can apply to.

Your knowledge of management is expanded by the training in accounting. You'll learn additional skills including people management and leadership.

6. *ACCA:*

- Eligibility:
  - Completed 10 + 2
  - An eligible CA is granted nine exemptions. So, only 4 professional level ACCA papers need to be attempted by qualified CAs. A CA can become an ACCA in 6–12 months.

- Areas of interest: Accounting, Finance, Auditing, Taxation
- Fees: Registration, subscription and exam fees add up to around £2,000
- Job Profiles:
  - Chief Financial Officer
  - Account Manager
  - Auditor
  - Finance Officer
  - Business Analyst
- Scope of ACCA + CA: Opportunity to work in BIG 4 and better opportunities to work abroad.
- The main reason I did ACCA was if I start practicing in the future, it will help fetch international clients easily.

7. *Actuarial Science*

- Eligibility: 10+2 pass for the Indian body; 10th Pass for the UK Body, need to have Mathematics as a subject in high school
- Exam pattern: Exams are conducted twice a year- April & September. 13 papers of which 10 are basic and 3 are specialized.
- Fees: Registration, subscription, and exam fees add up to Rs. 2-3 L
- Job roles:

  - Insurance
  - Financial Services
  - Life Insurance
  - Business/Investment Consulting
- Scope of CA + Actuarial Science: In Actuarial Science, you learn more about modelling, pricing, and valuation of products, and work in the insurance industry.
- The main reason I had enrolled in this course was my desire to stay in touch with mathematics and statistics. However, I quit after a point as I realized I didn't want to go in that direction. It was a personal choice.

8. *CFP*

- Eligibility: There are two types of eligibility here - Regular Pathway Eligibility or Challenged Status Pathway Eligibility
  - Under Regular Pathway Eligibility - you must have completed 10+2
  - Under Challenged Status Pathway Eligibility - you must have finished graduation or an equivalent degree (for direct entry)
- Area of Interest: Financial Planning, Money Management
- Exam Pattern: Conducted thrice a year - March,

July, November; 4 Modules to clear

- Exam Fees: Rs. 50,000 – 75,000. Can go upto Rs. 1 – 1.3 L including coaching fees, etc.
- Job Roles:
  - Personal Financial Planner
  - Wealth Management Advisor
  - Associate Advisor
  - Life Insurance
  - Small Business Consultancy

9. *CMT*

- Eligibility: Graduate degree expected
- Area of Interest: Technical Analysis
- Exam pattern: Conducted twice a year – June/July, November/December
- Fees: $1,500 – $2,000
- Job roles:
  - Portfolio Managers
  - Research Analyst
  - Market Product Trader
- Scope of CA+CMT: Enhances technical knowledge and widens job opportunities across domains. Improves research, report preparation, and analytical skills.

~

These are primarily the courses you can consider doing alongside or after CA. Note that this chapter is meant to give you just a preliminary understanding of such courses. If you're seriously considering pursuing any of them, I'd urge you to do in-depth research yourself and understand everything you can before taking the plunge.

Always remember: Don't enroll in any course just for the sake of collecting degrees and adding them to your badge! Enroll to gain skills and then apply them in the real world.

To be honest and blunt, after a point, your qualification will not matter. But your communication and application will! Focus more on gaining skills rather than running behind qualifications.

13. Learning from the Phoenix - Mr. T.N. Manoharan

If you've picked this book up, I'd be surprised if you don't know who Mr. T.N. Manoharan is. He is a Padma Shree awardee, a former president of ICAI, and an ex-Chairman of Canara Bank. He currently serves on the board of Mahindra & Mahindra, IDBI Bank, and National Bank for Financing and Infrastructural Development (NaBFID). He is credited for reviving the scandal-hit Satyam Computers in 2007, and has recently released his book 'The Tech Phoenix', which is an awe-inspiring account of the entire story.

I had the rare privilege of interviewing him for this book and got him to share his insights on Chartered Accountancy as a career and his suggestions for CA aspirants. Needless to say, with his perspectives stemming from decades worth of rich experience, this chapter is a goldmine for anyone looking to build a career as a CA.

With Mr. T.N. Manoharan at the launch of his book

The Beginning

Like every CA, there would have been a trigger which pushed Mr. Manoharan into this tough course. Turns out, fundamentally, it wasn't much different from most of us. Back in the 1970s, newspapers were the only way to check which jobs were in demand. Vacancies would be posted as 'Classified Ads', and he would skim through them daily to understand what the market wanted. He observed that three qualifications stood apart in terms of the number of openings: MBA, Cost Accountant, and CA. He was fascinated by them even though he had no idea about what they meant.

The final push came through when a family friend, Mr. Rajgopal, an industrialist and an MP then, suggested he choose CA over MBA. Mr. Manoharan recalls, "My father took me to visit him in Vellore. He told me clearly, 'In CA, you can either get a job or set up your own practice. Now, cracking CA is tough but once you have cracked it, you don't get to retire. You become an entrepreneur for life."

He added, "Two words which stuck with me were *tough* and *entrepreneur*. I love solving tough problems. And the fact that I don't have to seek a job, rather I'd be providing them had me enticed." We know from his career that he actually ended up doing really tough things and also helped create thousands of jobs.

Once the decision was made, he enrolled in a small

coaching center in Chennai. While it's easy to say "rest was history", he had his share of challenges right from the beginning. His command of English was poor and even got snide remarks from people for it. "Those who humiliate you, insult you, and provoke you, are the ones who actually mold you into a better version of yourself. Don't draw energy only from positive things, but from adverse situations too. The fire fueled by your critics won't let you rest until you have proved them wrong," he tells me.

Thanks to his hard work and the frequent remarks he'd cop that kept the fire burning and helped him pass CA successfully. His articleship was particularly arduous and left very little time for him to study. "I passed my CA finals but aiming for a rank wasn't even a possibility for me. I gave two groups together and appeared for the third group later. I could not take the pressure of taking up three groups together with the workload I had," he said.

Let's understand more about his ideas of what an ideal preparation approach for the entire curriculum should be.

Preparation Advice

Mr. Manoharan's first advice is about volume one, which should consistently be put into studying. He reckons that 10-12 hours is about the right amount of time one should put in daily to be fully prepared for the exams, depending upon the individual's grasping ability.

He has an even more elaborate suggestion for the preparation strategy. He says that the entire preparation should be broadly divided into 3 rounds, regardless of the exam and the subject.

Round 1 is about **familiarization** with the concepts. Just know the content, understand what goes where, intricacies, nuances, and difficulties you will have to face. Within this first round, divide the time spent on topics by categorizing them into three buckets.

- Bucket A: This is what comprises the major chapters, which are appearing in the paper and carry significant marks. You spend the most time in Bucket A.
- Bucket B: This bucket consists of topics and chapters that are important, but carry fewer marks than the ones in Bucket A. Spend some time in this bucket corresponding to their weightage in the curriculum.
- Bucket C: This bucket comprises those topics which are not frequently tested or carry very low weightage. Minimum time gets spent here.

"The benefit of this round is that you get to know something about everything. In my opinion, a student who knows something about everything would pass even in the most unexpected paper," Mr. Manoharan concludes about Round 1.

Round 2 is about **going deep** and slow into the classified topics. This is when you try to master the concepts. You might have attended coaching classes and this is the time when you assimilate the concepts that the faculty has taught you. After Round 1, you'd know exactly which topics need you to spend more time on and in what depth, so use your judgment to allocate time and energy accordingly.

Round 3 is about **revision**. The purpose is to tie up the loose ends. You know your Achilles heel by now, and it's now time to address them. He explains, "For example, if you open a chapter which you think are well-versed in, it may happen that you get stuck at one or two points and you may be able to fill it up from the textbook. But if you are stuck and keep on asking 'What next?', this means that you haven't mastered the subject yet. Then you devote more time to that topic and fill up the loose ends of your understanding. The moment all these three rounds are over, in a sense you are ready for the examination."

He adds further, "With this preparation strategy you achieve the required marks to pass the paper and scale up if the paper is in your comfort zone. Importantly, you are never taken by surprise."

But the preparation strategy doesn't stop at these three

rounds. He reckons that you should budget enough time for mock tests. He says:

"You need to finish your studies at least 20 days before your exam (e.g. if you are taking 8 subjects in your CA finals, 8 x 2 = 16 + 4 days for cushion). In those 20 days, you should also take at least two mock test papers. For your first round, start with Financial Reporting and end with Indirect Taxation. Take a two-day break to re-evaluate, gain confidence, and course correct. Then start the second round, beginning with Indirect Taxation and working your way back. This way, you should finish the first paper by October 29th and be ready for the real exam on November 1st. I used to follow this strategy so I would walk into the exam feeling like an experienced examinee." This, he believes, would drastically reduce the chance of failing any attempt because of a 'lack of experience'.

With the preparation strategy out of the way, I inquired Mr. Manoharan about the other big challenge aspirants face - managing studies along with the articleship.

Articleship and Preparation

Balancing articleship with your studies is tricky, but it doesn't mean that it is impossible. This tricky situation demands a solution, but opting for dummy articleship is cowardice. Dummy articleship is an easy way out which will only hurt you in the long run. If you opt for it, it means that you haven't in a true sense understood the importance of those three years. Mr. Manoharan elaborates, "The privilege you enjoy as a student is unique. You will not get that privilege after completing that articleship. Nobody will allow you in the office again with the same liberty and privilege. You will have constraints, conflict of interest, and confidentiality enforced upon you."

He further adds, "Articleship can help you gain practical insight and personal development. Don't just view it as a period of auditing and tax work; it's only a small part of the experience. Take advantage of interpersonal communication with your managers, colleagues, juniors, and clients. These activities will help you grow and refine yourself."

So, is there a solution? One way to improve learning is to transfer back to school days and adopt the school study approach. To test this hypothesis, he considered students who had passed both groups of CA interim exams. Just like in school, teachers used to give tests after finishing a topic; similarly, one could take weekly, monthly, and quarterly tests to reduce the burden of studying. "This is a volume course with a diversified subject. It's tough to pass it by rote learning. What is necessary is the application of the knowledge you gain. So students shouldn't wait for weekends to study. Rather they should have the discipline to study for one hour in the morning and one hour at night every day. This is the minimum benchmark."

But on weekends, he suggested studying for 6-8 hours. This approach ensures you are studying for fifteen to twenty hours a week. For the rest of the time, enjoy your articleship thoroughly. Completing two subjects in six months would lead you to complete all eight subjects in two years. To test your two subjects, borrow the question papers your seniors would be currently writing. In the last four months, adopt the practice of three rounds of reading as mentioned previously.

I was reading Mr. Manoharan's book 'The Tech Phonenix' in which he narrated an experience from his articleship journey. I think this incident beautifully sums up the importance of articleship and the different hues it adds to your personality. The following extract has been taken from his book:

> *This episode with Peter took my mind back to 1979. As an articled trainee, I accompanied my senior, K. Venkata Subbiah Naidu, to Mumbai for tax assessments. The tax offices were scattered across the city. My principal, then 80 years old, fell sick and wanted me to meet the commissioner of income tax (Appeals) at*

his Parel office and seek an adjournment. Instead of carrying just an adjournment letter, I spent the night preparing for the case like a full-fledged professional!

I reached the commissioner's office on time and was called in. When I explained the situation to him, he was furious.

"Do you know how many times your senior has sought a date change? I am going to pass an adverse ex parte order."

"Sir, I am well informed of the case, and if you permit, I can make the submissions!"

"Who are you?"

"I am an articled trainee with the firm, Sir?"

"What? You want me to hear out a trainee. Get out of my room'

I came out and waited. An hour later, the commissioner stepped out to use the restroom. When he returned, I stood beside his door and smiled. After going in, he rang the bell and asked me to come in. "Why have you not gone yet?"

"Sir, the client should not suffer, and my aged senior is unwell and unable to appear. If you can give me five minutes to recite the merits of the case, it would be helpful."

He reluctantly opened the file and I explained ground after ground, narrating facts and citing relevant prec-

edents. He heard me for over 45 minutes and asked a few questions, which I readily answered. He offered me a cup of tea at the end of it and wished me well for the exams.

A fortnight later, the client received a favourable order allowing the appeal in full.

The experience taught me an important lesson. In life, people may - due to circumstances, their stature or anxiety levels - belittle you. Do not take that to heart. Remember you are there to achieve a purpose. Focus on the purpose irrespective of how badly you get treated.

What a man! This attitude is what has led him to become one of the most successful CAs of our country. India is proud of him!

Now, that we have talked extensively about the articleship, let's hear about his major learnings from the CA curriculum.

Lessons from the CA Curriculum

Being a CA, Mr. Manoharan reckons, taught him the art of communication. CA is the one-stop answer to all the questions like "how to talk, what to talk, when to talk, and when to shut up". He says "With proper guidance and by making mistakes, I learned the instinct of when it's necessary to voice my opinions and when it is a smart choice to be silent." A good communicator doesn't just articulate their thoughts well but also listens intently and attentively, and CA teaches you that.

In a classroom filled with students of different backgrounds and caliber, the CA curriculum taught him patience and tolerance. Everyone is different. This diversity needs to be respected and we shouldn't disrespect people who are different from us. Everyone has their rhythm. He says, "With no discrimination, accommodate each one as they are."

But the hallmark lesson he says he learned was that of trust. CA profession is all about finance. It's a world of numbers. Hence, it is very important to understand the importance and sanctity of those numbers. Those numbers cannot leave the four walls of your office. It's when you have understood the importance of this that you can gain the trust of other people. "Anyone can discuss anything with me freely and it will not travel beyond me." When you are considered a confidant by your employers, your clients, and your colleagues, that's when you've mastered the trust factor.

He learned this lesson the hard way though. Once, it so happened that he shared a piece of information, something not too significant, about an international client with another client of his. Both clients knew each other. It was an ordinary slip of the tongue. When the client confronted him, he was left aghast. He understood then how important trust is and to not let the slightest of information out. Luckily, he learned this lesson at the very beginning of his career and was careful going forward.

Scope and Future of CA

Mr. Manoharan says the core area of Audit would remain in human hands for a long time to come. "We may have new gadgets, tools, analytics, and AI creeping in but all of these would only serve to assist the human mind in audits and not replace it. The professional judgment and skepticism which a seasoned professional brings to the table while executing an audit cannot be replicated by machines or an AI system. They can only serve to make the process efficient and/or cost-effective and hence should not be considered threats but supplementary ideas to the role of a CA."

He continunes, "Secondly, with faceless assessments and appeals, expectations from CAs are only rising. Even during a faceless assessment, the documents have to speak for themselves to get the desired result which is a skill in itself. New CAs can specialize in preparing ground appeals and other related documentation activities where without representation, the documents get a favorable order."

The Indian economy is growing, and with it, many

startups and MSMEs are entering the fray. This presents a great opportunity for upcoming CAs to provide virtual CFO services. Many MSMEs cannot afford a full-time CFO, so a CA with the necessary proficiency and competence can become a virtual CFO for multiple small firms at once. Additionally, they can help train the accounting departments of these organizations.

Business support services for foreign entities setting up industries and offices in India are becoming increasingly common. One of Mr. Manoharan's young acquaintances is now working in the USA as a part of the anti-money laundering division, providing services to major banking companies in America and global corporations. This team consists of 600 CAs working together. It is likely that in 5-10 years, India will also have a significant number of CAs working in similar departments.

Mr. Manoharan reckons that data privacy, cyber security, and other related fields are increasingly important domains for many companies and CAs with advanced skills and knowledge of these will have many takers.

He also advises young CAs to keep their goals high. He says, "For those who are joining jobs, you should not limit your goal to just becoming the head of the financial department. It's good to target becoming CFO, but gain management and leadership skills to even become the CEO. In my view, many CAs can become CEOs. If an MBA graduate can become a CFO or CEO of an organization, so can CAs. Two professionals can settle down anywhere in the world; technology and finance. These two are required for any economy. With the right experience and expertise, you can thrive anywhere."

Tech-savviness and Communication Skills

In this age of digitalization, technology skills and communication skills will be crucial for any CA entering the market. Technology is booming at a very rapid pace. Ten years down the line, it would have taken root in every industry. Mr. Manoharan says, "You'd just need to punch in the facts and you will get arguments for and against. Everything will be technologically driven." In such a world, being tech-savvy would be essential.

On communication, he remarks, "If you are not able to break the ice with someone in five minutes then you are not a good communicator. Somebody else will pitch in better and leave you behind." In his managers' conferences, he gives only 10 minutes for speakers to make their point which forces them to be crisp and brief while presenting ideas. Initially, his managers committed blunders. In ten minutes, they tried to include all twenty points they wanted to talk about. But with time, they improved and started communicating only the five most important points that made maximum impact.

He concluded on communication skills with this last thought: "In a boardroom, all the work that you have done may be sidelined. All that will matter is the introduction. If you can impress them with your introduction, you will set a good image in their mind. You would be seen as a mature and responsible person and then you can carry them along with you."

As we were nearing the end of the interview, I asked him one final piece of advice he would like to give to the CA students. This is the gem he shared at last: "Life is full of challenges and everyone has their limitations. Instead of being limited by your challenges, challenge your limitations. It's only then you will start attempting the impossible. You may fail at times, but you'd also create history with this attitude."

I hope my conversation with him helps you as much as it helped me. I will carry his illuminating words with me forever.

I also wrote a poem for him just to express my gratitude and respect. I hope you will like it. Turn over the page to read it.

Dear Sir,

You revived the mammoth giant Satyam because you are extremely *versatile*,
Your wife is a dentist, and that's the main reason behind your charming *smile*!

Spectators are awestruck and mesmerised whenever Sachin hits a *six*,
I had the same reaction, when I read your book, *'The Tech Phoenix'*!

For first few years of your career, you were also a CA *Practitioner*,
During articleship, kudos to your efforts in winning the case by waiting for 45 minutes outside the office of Income Tax *Commissioner*!

You are extremely patient and you've had several successful *stints*,
That's because you run at marathons and don't believe in *sprints*!

When you were awarded as Padma Shri, it was feeling of pride and *venerate*,
Loved your response to one of Executives, *"Like hard metals, my melting point is beyond the heat this fire can generate"*!

I am sure the satisfaction and relief would have been worth 100 days of *grind*,
Thanks for your amazing advice – take success to your heart and failure to the *mind*!

Solving taxation doubts of your students would now be easier than solving a Rubik's *cube*,
I was on the seventh heaven when you said you will appear on my channel on *YouTube*!

Our country needs more people like you named *Shri TN Manoharan*,
As of now, in India, there is only *one*! :)

- Kushal Lodha
(Your Mentee)

14. Parting Lessons from Mr. Dhiraj Khandelwal

CA Dhiraj Khandelwal is easily one of the most recognized faces among CA students as, among other reasons, he is the one who announces the result dates haha! Member of the Central Council of ICAI from 2016 to 2024, Mr. Khandelwal possesses wide experience in several areas. He's a veteran with over two decades across Business Advisory, Planning, Project Finance, FEMA, Cross Border Transactions, and Direct/Indirect Tax Consultancy.

Early Journey

Mr. Khandelwal belonged to a family of businessmen. After graduating with a B.Com, he decided to pursue

CA to help in his family business.

The journey of Dhiraj Khandelwal to becoming a CA was full of highs and lows. The biggest challenge he faced, like Mr. Manoharan, was the language barrier. Having studied in Hindi medium his whole life, seeing the ICAI syllabus in English gave him chills.

In the two and a half months of preparatory leave, he devoted more than 100% to his studies. Practical subjects like accounting, taxation, and costing were easy for him, as he was good at them. However, the theoretical subjects made him cry. But he persisted.

He made sure to read the entire syllabus three times. He studied for 13 hours a day without any distractions.

One common yet stupid mistake he reckons students make is that they try to find shortcuts in the journey. There is no escapism in CA. He says, "You must go through the complete study material. Don't leave anything. It's a wrong approach to prepare for only 70 marks out of 100." As a student, for the practice manual, he used to refer to some outside books. He himself ensured and still advises everyone to attempt and finish the exam papers from the last 10 years.

Like all other successful people, he has also faced setbacks. Despite appearing for both groups in the CA Interim exam, he only passed Group 1. Did this make him give up? No. It only made him try harder. What kept him motivated and upbeat? Fulfilling his parents' dream was one, and the second was the example set by his seniors whom he wanted to emulate. Out of the 300 students living in the RVG hostel, where he used to stay, only 4-5 people failed the CA exam. He re-appeared for Group 2 after six months and not only did he pass, he scored more than 70 marks in all the subjects. During his time, the acceptance rate of CA was only 1%. His dedication earned him a spot in that exclusive group.

This rollercoaster journey taught him some key lessons. Hard work and persistence were emphasized early, instilling in him a never-give-up attitude. Balancing study with articleship taught him the importance of consistency. These basic lessons helped him persevere through many daunting challenges in life.

But is CA even worth such efforts? What does CA offer that makes the journey worthwhile?

Opportunities for CAs

CAs have a bright and opportune future in India, he reckons. The scope of CAs ranges across business, corporate jobs, and one's own practice. Modern-day practices are unlike traditional practices, and offer ample opportunities across domains.

In terms of jobs too, the highest roles aren't limited to that of the CFO. He said, "I know 76 people who are CEOs of various companies. 30-40 of my own batchmates have their businesses and they are performing really well. After doing CA, one could also go into the field of HR, sales, and operations. It is no longer restricted to the accounting department only."

One can also do post-grad courses like MBA. Not just that, Mr. Khandelwal knows of 6 CAs who did another bachelor's degree after CA to enter fields like artificial intelligence. Moreover, CAs are also leaving their mark in civil services as IAS, IPS, and IRS officers.

In terms of opportunities outside India, Mr. Khandelwal recalls, "On my visit to London, I met a few of my connections and they told me that there are a lot of opportunities in the UK for CAs. Furthermore, India has signed a pact with the UK where 3,000 graduate students would get job visas for two years in either of the countries. We are soon going to have similar pacts with EU too."

Mr. Khandelwal, like Mr. Manoharan, is bullish that the scope and opportunities for CAs make the degree worth a shot. Next, I enquired about other important courses and skills CA students can consider.

What Else with CA?

ICAI very well understands that change is the only constant. It offers a lot of post-grad courses in all areas like valuation, forensics, blockchain technology, and even CSR. ICAI also gives certificate courses in startups. He said, "One can access all the information regarding these courses under the digital learning tab on the ICAI website."

As we move forward, anyone who doesn't embrace technology will become redundant. Mr. Khandelwal advises that it's a great idea to undertake courses that help you understand the basics of new-age technologies better.

On management skills, ICAI provides several courses that are similar to MBA. He informs, "ICAI has tied up with IIM Ahmedabad and signed an MOU with Harvard University for several management-related programs. They will become operational by this year (2023) or next year (2024)."

ICAI Incubation Cell

Like IITs, ICAI too, has come up with an incubation cell. The first one came about in 2018 in Mumbai. But due to the pandemic, they could not get much done. This year (2023), they plan to open 15 incubation centers. MOU has been signed with IIM Lucknow, I-Hub Gujarat government, and the BSE stock exchange.

Elaborating on the incentives of these incubation cells, he said, "Earlier too, ICAI had incubation centers, but they were not connected to the government. Through I Hub, BSE, and IIT, they will get more funding (depending on the criteria of state-to-state funding). In these incubation cells, students get to learn under excellent mentors such as Mr. Motilal Oswal. Furthermore, they have funding programs where they learn how to pitch to investors, understand the nuances of starting up, and get access to resources that can help them grow faster.

I have been requested by a lot of students to ask Mr. Khandelwal about the path to become a Central Council Member of ICAI, so I requested him to elaborate on that.

Central Council Membership

To become a CCM, there is a ladder to climb. It begins with becoming an active member in ICAI conferences and seminars. He told me, "The decision whether you become a CCM or not depends on the people. They gain power through voting, so they must be able to see and recognize your work. Your attitude towards other members and students is also important."

He suggested joining a study circle for starters. This will make the 200-300 members of the group your family. You always love your family and want to serve them. The next step is becoming the secretary, then chairman. Finally, you will reach the last rung, which is becoming a member of the Central Council.

He recalled his own journey: "In 2006, I became a Regional Council member. I was a member for 9 years. In 2014, I stood for the Central Council and got elected. Note that this was more than 10 years after serving the community. In 2021, I was re-elected and this is my third and last term."

Becoming a member of any society is a way to serve its members. Those who feel they have the capacity to serve the CA community should strive to become a CCM, or even aim higher and become the President of ICAI. This position comes with great responsibility, but also with its rewards. "You become the leader of those same professors who have given you so much. This is an opportunity to give them back."

ICAI's Growth

The ICAI is growing and will continue to do so in the future. In the past, ICAI was limited to auditing only. However, in the last decade, this has changed drastically. He said, "ICAI is now more credible in every government sector. It is involved in drafting rules and regulations, and the government is seeking detailed information from ICAI."

ICAI is now the world's largest body in accounting

and the second-largest body globally. In the next two to three years, it is expected to become the largest body in the world. He further elaborated, "ICAI is now being recognized globally, even more so after hosting the world congress. People in the IFAC body are looking up to us as a technical hub, as we have developed digitally. ICAI is a leader in sustainable development, which is the way forward for the world. We used to follow the footsteps of our western counterparts, but now we are marking our own footsteps, which are being followed by the rest of the world."

~

Before bidding Mr. Khandelwal goodbye, I asked him for a final piece of advice for the readers of the book. He did me a favour and gave me two pieces of advice instead. The first was about where young CAs should increasingly look to work.

He reckons that with time, it's becoming more and more necessary to have well-rounded skills than just being good with finance and numbers, as the CA curriculum teaches. Contrary to what most CA students desire, Mr. Khandelwal suggests that more students should now look forward to working at startups as they'd learn multiple things at once. He says, "Everyone does their articleship for three years so they anyway have the basic CA knowledge from there. I suggest students should work at startups for 2-3 years. Working in a startup would give them an opportunity to learn marketing, sales, product, give them a better business context, and help them understand how to use social media for the company's brand and their own."

His final piece of advice was about being grateful for the country we live in and that everyone should give back in some form. He said, "Now that you have become a CA, it's time for you to give back to the country. We take pride in calling ourselves the CA army for economic growth. And as its soldiers, we must combine to develop the economic health of our country. We should do our absolute best to help our clients and employers do better, but through all this, we must always work with complete honesty and integrity."

~

Let me share something interesting. Whenever I received any official communication from The Institute of Chartered Accountants of India, there would be an address that read:

"ICAI Bhawan, Indraprastha Marg, New Delhi"

I often wondered how it would be in reality and what

if I get a chance to visit my own alma mater which has led me to achieve whatever little I have.

That dream turned into reality in July 2022. It was only because of Mr. Dhiraj Khandelwal that I could experience this moment. I have never seen such a humble and down-to-earth person. People like him are a pure source of inspiration for all the students and young entrepreneurs. His vision for the benefit of students is just amazing.

For some people, happiness is earning billions of dollars. For others, it is getting fame or recognition. For me, it is visiting your own prestigious Institute and contributing in any manner whatsoever in future projects.

15. It's Just the Beginning!

I come from an entrepreneurial background and had the seeds of entrepreneurship sown in me all along. My stint at Aditya Birla Group only made my resolution stronger. I met thousands of founders, came across a plethora of ideas, and understood the needs of the market. Becoming a CA and doing a job was like providing nourishment to the seed. It was now time to take the plunge into building something of my own.

It does not mean the decision of quitting my job at ABG was easy. I still remember the number of conversations I had with my mentors and colleagues before taking the big call. After all these interactions, I realized that ultimately, you should follow what your heart says and do what you think is right for you.

I had the safety net of income from content creation and my dad's real estate business as a backup option. Therefore, it was easier for me to make the decision as compared to someone without such privileges! Therefore, just because someone else has quit their job or is doing something different, don't follow simply because it appears cool or courageous. Everyone has different circumstances that factor in all the crucial decisions of their lives. And the tricky bit is people get to know whether the decision was correct or not only after the decision is made and lived through. If you become super successful after quitting your job, it will be hailed as the best decision ever, but if you struggle to find success, you'll be made an example of it for all the wrong reasons.

In the end, my advice is simple: do what you think is best for you without worrying too much about the future. If you're passionate about something, have the right skills to make a living, and are willing to put in the hours, you can have a comfortable life. Don't overthink it; just do what feels right.

Ultimately, everything turns out well in the end! If it's not okay, it's not the end.

~

A successful person once asked me, "What is your priority right now?", and I answered, "Money".

They said I didn't have my priorities set and I'd realize this in a few years. I agree, but I also disagree. At the young age of early twenties, I aspire for financial freedom and want to create a safety net for myself. Once I reach a stage where I'm not worried about money, it won't be my priority. My framework is to use my time to make money and use that money to make up for the time I lost.

The CA curriculum has given me a lot. It has built and enhanced qualities that have prepared me to face the real world. One of the biggest lessons it has taught me is that I am responsible for my own actions. It has prevented me from becoming a victim of the 'excusitis' disease - a mental condition where a mediocre person makes excuses for every situation.

I have made many mistakes in my life (some of which I have shared in the book), and I take full responsibility for them. I don't view failure as an end, but rather as an experience from which I can learn and move on.

The curriculum and studying for twelve hours a day taught me to be patient. This patience, in turn, enabled me to remain level-headed in times of crisis. During my CA journey and corporate life, I often had to make decisions quickly in the face of a crisis. In those moments, it was essential to stay calm and composed. If I had panicked, I wouldn't have been able to make the right choices.

I learned the art of self-discipline during those five years. Although it can be boring, it is always successful. I'm so used to following a routine now that I feel uneasy when it's disrupted. The only difference now is that I understand dedicating twelve hours a day to work is neither healthy nor necessary. Smart work is the key; effectively working eight hours is enough. The rest of the day should be devoted to other important things like health, personal growth, and family.

At 18, the CA curriculum taught me to prioritize my time and find balance in life. Managing work and studies has not only taught me how to manage my personal and professional life but also how to take time for myself. This is a quality that is essential in the real world. Thanks to this skill, I was able to create and manage my side hustle without it taking a toll on me.

~

As children, we were often told that putting 100% effort into a task at a particular stage would make the rest of our lives a breeze. We heard this in 10th grade when we took our board exams, again in 12th grade, and again while pursuing CA. I'm sure you've been told that if you work hard for just these five years, life ahead would be a piece of cake. But honestly, there's no truth in this, none at all. After reaching a certain goal, not working hard is a choice you can make. But remember, while living leisurely in your comfort zone may give you a comfortable life after CA, it would never lead to rapid growth that eventually makes people exceptional. After the degree, we obtain freedom, but that freedom comes with responsibilities and higher expectations. If you desire to do exceptional things, you'll have to continue working on yourself to become better every day.

That's why I believe that it's good to stay dissatisfied and have that constant hunger to achieve more in life. If I became satisfied with my CA qualification, I would never have enrolled for the CFA course. Or if I had become content with my ranks in CA Foundation and Intermediate, I would never have worked hard to get a rank in CA Finals. I could do it because I was dissatisfied and aspired for something bigger in my life.

Of course, you should celebrate your small achievements just like a kid who gets an ice-cream. But when you're done celebrating, it's time to focus on the next big thing. Everything is relative in nature and you will constantly compare with the next best person to become like them. Once you outperform them, you will then again compare with the next person above. This is a constant loop and doesn't end until you are satisfied. Being satisfied, in my opinion, is a sign of not striving for more. I'd say, ***be proud but not satisfied!***

~

I'm proud to call myself a CA, but my identity isn't limited to this degree and the academic knowledge I gained. It has instilled in me the ability to face any challenge, and I use that ability every day as I build my own brand and business now. Anyone can learn theoretical stuff online today, but few things teach grit and resilience like the CA journey.

That's why becoming a CA is not the end. It should never be. You have already been equipped to do so much! You have already shown that you're capable to do hard things. When you finish CA, you embark on a new journey. It's different from the one you took for the previous five years or more, and it's up to you how beautiful you can make it.

That's why I say that the end of CA is just the beginning of a new chapter. *Kyunki picture abhi baaki hai mere dost!*

Acknowledgements

Every CA student goes through a lot of confusion, doubt, and even pain throughout their preparation journey. It ranges from the reasons for enrolling in the CA course, methods to study consistently and efficiently, articleship, and most importantly, what to do after becoming a Chartered Accountant.

Instead of answering each question individually on different forums, why not compile them into a book where I can also share some relatable life experiences to help students move forward and act as a guiding light on their journey! That's how the idea of *Acing CA* was born, and it's my small way of giving back to the CA community. Special thanks to Vedant Johari for giving me the idea of writing this book.

This book would not have been possible without the constant support of my parents. It's because of them that I cleared my exams in the first place. My dad has been the biggest motivator and my mom - my constant support system!

A heartfelt thanks to Yashraj Sharma, Prishita Tahilramani, and the team at Wyzr for their immense help in writing the book. I dreamt, and they executed :)

Thanks to Om Kedia for helping me with some research points regarding the statistics mentioned.

A big thank you to Shayan Gooneratne, Aayushi Gupta and Prasanna Surana for their critical and invaluable feedback on my early drafts. Their suggestions made the book so much better.

Also, special thanks to Mr. Deepak Parekh, Mr. Suresh Prabhu, Mr. TN Manoharan, Dr. Ajit Ranade, Mr. Ashwin Damera, Ms. Rachana Ranade, Sharan Hegde, Anant Ladha, and Sarthak Ahuja for endorsing this book through their valuable words!

Finally, thank you, my reader, for trusting me enough to pick this book up. I hope this serves the purpose you picked it for.

Now that you've read it, I'd love to know your thoughts and feedback at ksl@kushallodha.in!